Loving
MY WIFE

IN SICKNESS & IN HEALTH

THE LOVE STORY OF
EPHRAIM & SYLVIA JONES

Loving
MY WIFE

IN SICKNESS & IN HEALTH

THE LOVE STORY OF
EPHRAIM & SYLVIA JONES

EPHRAIM JONES

Written by: A. Felicity Darville

UNIVERSAL IMPACT PRESS

Contents

Preface

Sitting here in our home, a place now filled with memories and echoes of a life we built together, I'm telling our story to someone who can put it into words better than I ever could. This ain't just any story; it's a real-life testament of what it meant for me and my wife to go through the rollercoaster that life threw at us.

This book, it's my heart laid out in words, a tribute to my wife, a woman of extraordinary strength and love. I'm sharing our journey, a real look at the ups and downs of being husband and wife through the toughest of times. It's about showing what true commitment looks like, and man, it's more than most folks ever realize.

As you read through these pages, you'll get a front-row seat to our life, the good times and the hard ones. It's more than just sharing memories; it's about honoring a woman who was the backbone of our family, and a testament to sticking together no matter what life throws your way.

So here I am, recounting the moments that made us who we are, starting from those times when we were hit hardest, but stood strong together. This story, our story, it's about the love and the bond that held us tight, a bond that's as strong now as ever, living on in our hearts, and the legacy she's left behind.

As I watched my wife lying down and not being able to do much, and I had to take her to the bathroom, I had to bathe her, sometimes three, four times a night. As time went on, I said to myself you know something, I have to share this story so people can understand that there's more to being husband and wife than people really think it is.

Then I start hearing about marital rape and men not being there for their families and that type of stuff. I keep hearing women saying it is more about women than anything else, I keep trying to figure out if they had any understanding of what good men, committed men go through.

Everybody just talks about this and that, when I see and hear about people they give awards to all the time for this, that, and the next, they don't realize what two people who are nurtured properly together do in a society.

I always put my children as a prime example. I said you know, I have got to tell this story, because here it is, I have two excellent young men and we always talk negatively about our young men. I have two excellent young men and although people see that and they are well respected in society, people are not getting close to them to find out. They say "You boys are similar to your dad or you boys are so good; tell me how you got to this."

I decided that I was going to write a book to talk about my wife because she was so committed and dedicated. She was just excellent. What could you say about somebody who was just above and beyond at all times? She was super good. She took care of our family.

I watched her during her sickness say to my son, "Dad is coming over. He likes the soup that you normally get... broccoli soup." He would buy that and my wife would sit down or lie down and refuse to eat until I came. And when I came, that smile... the minute I open the door, that smile is just bursting open! She would say, 'Ron, get the food, so dad can get something to eat because I know he is tired and hungry. I don't normally eat when I am traveling. She knows that because that's how it is with us. We normally eat together. So when I get there, she hops out of the bed, or if she is sitting down she stands up and we go in the kitchen. And she says, 'You eat'.

We never ate out of two different plates, you know. We share one plate all the time. I would eat some, she would eat some. And that's how we were. I couldn't help but want to tell her story. Because here it is, a story about an excellent wife and then it's a story about wonderful children. Then it's a story about a husband who made sure he was committed to her because of what she did for him. She was second to none.

Writing this book, I feel compelled to share her story, to celebrate her remarkable life and the indelible mark she left on us. Her legacy is a beacon of what it means to love selflessly, and to stand by each other through the most challenging times. This book is more than a tribute to her; it's a call to others to understand the depth and resilience of true love, especially in the face of adversity.

Her story is one of courage, of grace under pressure, and of the unbreakable bond of marriage. It's about the power of being there for each other, in sickness and in health, until the end.

By sharing this, I hope to inspire others to embrace these values, to recognize the beauty in commitment, and to cherish every moment with their loved ones.

My wife's legacy is a reminder of the strength found in love and partnership, a legacy that deserves to live on and guide others in their own journeys.

Foreword

When Mr. Ephraim Jones invited me to work with him on this book, I did not know that he would impact my life the way he did. As a writer, I enjoy telling the stories of people who are doing extraordinary things. These may be subtle things - things that could easily be taken for granted. But when we slow the wheels of our lives down, just enough to pay more attention, we discover just how great the little things are. They are everything! We help build humanity by our love and care for others. So while Mr. Jones could have been considered just a man doing what he should - loving his family and engaging in positive enterprise - a closer look reveals much more.

Ephraim is a man who has embodied what a fine husband and father should be. He has poured out his entire spirit into his family, and has showered them with all the love in his being.

In this day and age, it seems that many could learn from his lesson in order to save their families, their marriages and their homes. He is the quintessential husband and father. Some marvel at him and wonder how he was able to do it all. I don't think he even knows. When you operate from a place of pure love, anything can happen.

In his case, the very best happened. He met the woman of his dreams, Sylvia, married her, and created a beautiful family with her. They were inseparable.... that is until death parted them.

When Ephraim lost Sylvia, he lost a big chunk of himself. Her battle with cancer was a difficult journey, but she remained the beautiful, caring, happy woman she was until the end. During her battle, Ephraim took care of his wife like a baby. He never hired anyone to fulfill his role. He learned the meaning of loving his wife in sickness and in health, as he vowed to do on his wedding day. It was an arduous task, but he faced it with resolve and determination to give his wife the best possible life every day that she was alive.

Ephraim shares this book to celebrate the memory of the most phenomenal woman he ever met; his life partner; best friend; mother of his children; his confidante and everything in between.

But he also shares this book for you. If you are a caregiver, especially a spouse having to love the person they married as they fight cancer, you will be motivated and comforted by Ephraim's testimony.

If you are a husband or wife, you will be touched to love your spouse even more and in better ways, like I have.

If you are just a reader, you will be inspired by a love story that is one for the ages.

Enjoy!

A. Felicity Darville

Chapter 1

Island Virtues

Roots in the Bahamas: The Foundation of Character

THE BENEFITS OF A good old-fashioned Bahamian upbringing cannot be overlooked. There's something special about the little island girl or boy fashioned by the hands and hearts of parents with high moral values and an appreciation for the simple things in life. Love, family, togetherness, forgiveness, encouragement, and patience... all great virtues that were nurtured in the home of Ephraim Jones.

Alfred Alpheus Jones and Alice Melita Jones raised a fine young man. Their example of faithfulness to God and commitment to each other was mirrored in their son Ephraim's marriage to Sylvia Jones (née Minns). Through their life example, Ephraim successfully navigated life with a heart full of love and gratitude.

Island Life and Its Influence

Alfred was born in Mayaguana, The Bahamas. It is the easternmost island in the beautiful archipelago, surrounded by shallow waters rippling in the most fascinating blue hues. Mayaguana is known for its fertile soil, meaning the islanders - a very small population - spent their days fishing and farming, living off the land.

They knew what it was to be far and isolated. But their circumstances led to the development of a tightly-knit community filled with love.

Alice was born in Acklins, another far-flung island in The Bahamas with a small population. Fishing is important to these people, but they also have a rare commodity. Acklins is one of only two islands in The Bahamas where the cascarilla bark is found. The essential oil derived from the cascarilla bark is highly desired and sought after. It is used for flavoring aperitifs, liquors (such as Campari), beverages, confections, and fine perfumery.

The archipelagic nature of The Bahamas has resulted in a series of closely-knit communities. They are made up of God-fearing people who love the land and sea. They respect each other and teach their children that manners and respect will take them around the world. That is exactly what happened. Bahamians can be found excelling in every corner of the globe.

A New Life in Nassau

Alfred and Alice made their way to Nassau, New Providence - the capital. Many Family Islanders did so on a quest to empower themselves further. The enterprising Alfred carved his own path to employment as a painter and also as a fish man. Back in the day, the fish man would have a cart and travel to various neighborhoods selling fresh seafood. By having two sources of income, Alfred was able to take care of his family.

Alice brought her wonderful Acklins-style cooking skills to Nassau. She improved them by taking a course for cooks. Classes were held at the place we now call the Dundas Center for Performing Arts. Long before it became the theater it is known as today, it was a training school for people interested in working in hospitality and other industries - similar to the National Training Center we have today.

Influential Connections: The Lindroths

Alice became a cook for one of the most influential families in Nassau, who adored the meals she created from the heart. She worked for the Lindroths - a family that made a meaningful impact on The Bahamas.

Arne Lindroth was the right-hand man for Axel Wenner-Gren in Switzerland. He was an industrialist and one of the richest men in the world in the 1930s. Wenner-Gren amassed a fortune from his early insight that the industrial vacuum cleaner could be adapted for domestic use. Wenner-Gren had bought much of Hog Island in The Bahamas in the late 1930s as a possible retreat in case of war with Hitler. He sent his trusted right-hand Arne Lindroth to oversee the development of Hog Island. Arne left Switzerland and arrived in Nassau in 1951. A year later, his wife, Gunnel, joined him, along with their three sons, Ulf, Orjan, and Magnus, who was just 14 months old when they arrived. Later on, their fourth child and only daughter, Elizabeth, would be born.

Arne Lindroth led the development of Hog Island into Paradise Island. This became the foundation of a world-renowned tourist destination that still attracts millions of people to this day. Wenner-Gren also commissioned Lindroth to spearhead the development of Lighthouse Point in Fresh Creek, Andros. Lindroth also spent time as the director of Bank of Bahamas (which is now known as Bank of The Bahamas). Orjan followed in his father's footsteps and, as an architect, laid out the framework for the development of two thriving communities in The Bahamas - Old Fort Bay and Schooner Bay.

Growing Up with the Lindroths

Ephraim grew up with the Lindroth children and was like a brother to them. He was an only child in his home. His elder sister, Gladys, whom his father had before his marriage to Alice, was much older. Magnus Lindroth would later recall that Alice was a "real Bahama mama" and the best cook in the world.

Even though the Joneses moved to the city, they continued to work diligently and never lost their island values. In their home, they nurtured Ephraim and gave him the best life they could, knowing that the ultimate lesson he should learn is to love his neighbor as himself, as Christ commanded.

Educational Journey and Scouting Adventures

When it came time for schooling, Ephraim first attended Holy Spirit Pre School in Chippingham where Father Humes was Rector. This Holy Spirit foundation laid a path for Ephraim that boded well for his life. He went on to attend St. Mary's Pre-School before going to Quarry Mission School for the beginning of his primary school education. Once he completed Quarry Mission Primary, he attended the Tan and Brown School. The school was not specifically named for a long time. Many great Bahamians attended this school, which was simply known by the colors of its uniform.

He then attended Western Junior, where Mr. Bowleg was the principal at the time. After completing Western Junior, he went on to Western Senior, led by Principal Glover, followed by Principal Huyler. After Western Senior High School, he attended Oakes Field Secondary School, followed by the newly built John F. Kennedy School, later named H.O. Nash, where he graduated.

Ephraim had the privilege of being trained as a young Boy Scout. By the time he graduated high school, Ephraim had moved up the ranks of the Boy Scouts. He was diligent in completing challenge after challenge. He mentored the boys younger than him, showing them the path to excellence that he followed. The Boy Scouts Association aims to produce Scouts that are: "trustworthy, loyal, helpful, friendly, courteous, kind, obedient, cheerful, thrifty, brave, clean, and reverent". Ephraim's character was shaped by these tenets, leading to a deep bond with the Scouts Association that continues to this day.

When Ephraim left school, he was a part of the 8th Bahamas Scout Troop that met at Trinity Methodist Church. The Scout Master was Ken Lloyd. One Friday night when Ephraim was attending their scheduled Scout Troop meetings, Mr. Lloyd asked Ephraim what he planned to do now that he had graduated high school. When the young Ephraim told him that he was looking for a job, Mr. Lloyd exclaimed, "Well look no more!"

He sent Ephraim to the One Hour Photo Lab on Thompson Boulevard opposite the National Sports Center of The Bahamas. The lab was run by the Lofthouse Group. He was to ask for Brian Eccleston.

Bright and early that Monday morning, the 17-year-old Ephraim went, neatly dressed, with high hopes of getting a job at the One Hour Photo Lab. There, he met Ben Knowles, who introduced him to the broom and the mop. Ephraim immediately started cleaning up the lab, happy that he had landed his first job.

What the staff at the One Hour Photo Lab did not know was that the young teenage boy hired to clean up would become one of the most outstanding photographers in the country. They did not know that he would climb the ranks from a seemingly unclimbable position, to manage the store, knowing the ins and outs of every intricate part of the business. They did not know he would be the one to rise up and train others - especially when, for the most part, he trained himself.

Ephraim did not know that this job would train him just as much. Here, he would grow into a fine man... and here, he would meet the love of his life.

Chapter 2

The Laboratory of Life

A New Era in The Bahamas

E PHRAIM JONES WAS 17 years old when he landed his first
job at the One Hour Photo Lab. It was around the year
1967, coinciding with the year that Majority Rule took place in
The Bahamas.

On January 10th, 1967, a General Election was held, marking
the first time the government transitioned from minority rule to
Majority Rule. This signified a shift from the old Bahamas to a new
Bahamas and a transition to modern democracy.

Six years later, on July 10, 1973, The Bahamas would become an
independent nation.

Transitioning with His Nation

While the country transitioned to independence, Ephraim was transitioning from boyhood to manhood. His parents were among the many black Bahamians who exercised their right to vote and change the trajectory of their country's future.

Ephraim's mother, Alice, gained this right to participate in the nation's elections back in 1962, thanks to the tireless advocacy of the Bahamas Women's Suffrage Movement. Women's right to vote went hand in hand with the right for all black men to vote. Previously, a man had to own property to participate in the General Elections.

It was on July 13, 1959, that a new General Assembly Elections Act was passed, finally removing the property qualifications for men to vote. Universal adult suffrage was passed in the House of Assembly in 1961.

Ambition at the Photo Lab

Ephraim was prepared to work hard at the One Hour Photo Lab to earn his income. But he was not prepared to stay as the janitor. He saw some opportunities for advancement. He could have very well continued cleaning the store every day and going home, content to collect his paycheck until something better came along.

Instead, he carved his own path to success right where he was. While cleaning up, Ephraim would come across some big, heavy books in the photo lab. These were books on photo printing procedures.

At the time, the One Hour Photo Lab was the only place that developed and printed photos. Therefore, photographers throughout the country brought their negatives there to be developed.

Learning from Every Opportunity

Ephraim would take the books home at night and read them. One by one, he would take home a "Bible" on photo printing, as he called them. He would read these books, take notes, and any time he came upon information that he thought was vital, he would pull out a voice recorder that he had. He would read the excerpts aloud.

Sometimes, Ephraim fell asleep reading with the recorder still on.

A Critical Moment of Truth

Ephraim's experience occurred about a decade before Koum was even born. As Ephraim returned each book, he relied on his faithful recorder to play back that information and let it soak into his brain. The moment of truth had come for Ephraim. He and Brian Eccleston went to the back of the store to the darkroom where the photos were developing. Mr. Eccleston took Ephraim's roll of prints and loaded it on the machine for processing. Then, they went to the front of the store where the printing machine takes the photos from the dark area to the light. Mr. Eccleston was so amazed at his work that Ephraim eventually became a part of the printing team.

Mastering the Craft

None of the workers at the photo lab liked mixing the chemicals involved in photo development. The chemistry room was up high in the store, and Ephraim would go up there and mix the chemicals. Then, he would go into the darkroom to print. He would load up the 100ft roll of paper and heat the paper to join the pieces together. The paper would then be pulled through a chemical solution, and the finished product - a developed photograph, would come out. This lab printed for all the photographers on the island.

The Journey to Independence

Ephraim's tenacity paid off. He was eventually selected to attend a course in Rochester, New York, USA, Kodak Headquarters. Ephraim eventually became a supervisor of the photo lab. He spent ten years with that company. When he left, Ephraim had the skills and knowledge to open up his own company. He opened up his own photo lab on Wulff Road.

Chapter 3

Love at First Sight

A Captivating Photograph

Ephraim's daily practice of developing photos made him a pro. He enjoyed his work immensely. He had the opportunity to see the development of The Bahamas on film. All of the most significant events of the day, captured on camera, were developed at his workplace.

Among these were photographs of the beauties of the day, but one photo, in particular, caught his eye. It was a photo taken by the noted photographer Antoine Ferrier.

"He took a beautiful photo of her," Ephraim said. "I said to the clerk, 'I don't know who this young lady is, but put these photos aside; I need to meet her.'"

The Five-Day Wait

"I was 26 when I met Sylvie. She came to the lab to see if her prints were ready." "I saw this girl; she had a beautiful smile.

I said to her, 'We're having problems with the machine'. I told her that she would have to come back in a couple of days, and that she should leave her number. Even though she did not get her photograph, she was still very pleasant."

"As she walked away, I said to the clerk, 'I am getting married to that girl; she won't escape me.'"

First Impressions

Sylvia Minns had left a contact for her place of work. She was a teller at the Royal Bank of Canada.

When Ephraim called her, he told her the photograph still wasn't ready, but that he was doing due diligence and following up. "But you promised me," Sylvia said. "Yet this is another day, and my picture isn't ready."

What struck Ephraim is that despite the ridiculously long wait, Sylvia was still gracious and polite. He assured her that he would personally deliver her the photograph.

This time, he scored her home phone number.

Lunch Invitations and Bread Pudding

Ephraim waited until that Saturday to call Sylvia. She would be free from work then and hopefully, he would have a chance to speak with her. He called to let her know that he had the photograph, and that he would be personally delivering it to her.

As bold as he was to hold off on giving her the photo, nerves got the best of him when it came time to make this personal delivery. She gave him directions to her home on Fifth Street.

'I drove down through Fifth Street; I saw the house," he said. "The front door was open. You could see people in the house, sitting at the dining room table.

I went to the corner of Fifth Street and Robinson Road. I turned back around and drove slowly by the house, then went back up to the corner again. When I went up the second time, I had enough courage and nerve to go to the house. I just waved and said hello."

Agnes, her sister, came outside. Ephraim told her he was looking for Sylvia Minns. Agnes went inside to call her. As Ephraim stood at the door, he could hear someone in the house say, "There's a gentleman out here to see you. Stop cutting up and go outside!"

When she came to the door, Ephraim's heart skipped a beat. He was timid, not knowing what to say. She was just as beautiful as ever. Although she was at home, she was nicely dressed - even in her house clothes.

She was wearing an apron, so Ephraim asked her if she was cooking. She said no, that she was baking. Ephraim asked for a piece of whatever she was baking.

She told him that he surely could, but that it wasn't ready yet, and he would have to come back. Of course, that was no problem for Ephraim. He gave her the photograph and left.

Sylvia had a lovely family- a big family. What Ephraim didn't know is that he dodged a bullet when Agnes came to the door and not Sylvia's father.

He was a big, burly man, at least 6'3" in height, with a big, hearty voice. His presence alone was intimidating, and with Ephraim already being nervous, things could have gone quite differently.

Lucky for him, things went smoothly and he had scored an opportunity to see her twice in one day.

To kill time, Ephraim drove out to Long Wharf by the beach, near Smiley's restaurant. He sat on the beach until about 5 pm, then made his way back to the Minns residence. He took a slow drive there, making sure he gave her enough time.

When he returned, Sylvia gave him a piece of what she had made - a delicious slice of bread pudding. He thanked her for it. The beach must have helped his nerves to drift away because he built up the courage to make his appeal.

He said: "Can I treat you to lunch next week?" She responded positively.

Conversations and Confessions

Ephraim started his work week as usual, but there was something different - thoughts of the beautiful Sylvia flooded his mind.

He picked up the phone three or four times on Monday to call her, but he hung up. Once again, nerves were getting the best of him.

He called on Tuesday, but he was too late. Sylvia already had lunch. So that Wednesday, he brought her lunch. She worked at Royal Bank in Palmdale. He bought her food from a restaurant called Banana Boat, which he said had the best food in those days.

When Ephraim arrived at Royal Bank in Palmdale, he went to the entrance and asked the security officer to take the lunch over to Sylvia Minns. The officer took the lunch from him and delivered it to her. She looked up and waved. He waved back and then immediately darted out of the bank.

Ephraim recalls: "The way I dashed out of that place, you would swear someone was running me!" "I didn't have the nerve or the guts to say anything."

Later on, he called and asked her if she enjoyed the meal. She asked him why he hadn't come in to speak with her.

On Thursday, he called her at home so that they could have the opportunity to have a proper conversation. That was the beginning of what would become a lifetime of conversation between two souls who had found their true love.

"From the moment I physically saw her, I said wow, this is someone I am not going to let go of," Ephraim said. "Here it is, I was a young fella, with no intention of getting married. She changed the whole narrative. It was love at first sight."

Chapter 4

The King and Knights

Struck by Beauty and Patience

E PHRAIM WAS STRUCK BY Sylvia's beauty. But he was also impressed with her sweet and patient nature. He recalls the day she came to the photo lab looking for her photo.

"She was beautiful. She was sparkling, and so pleasant. Even though she couldn't get her photos that day." Ephraim would learn later on that Sylvia would carry that sparkling and pleasant nature with her throughout her entire life.

A Fortunate First Impression

"Even when I first visited her house, and she was in her kitchen attire, she was still beautiful," he said. "She still caught my eyes.

Her dad wasn't at home on that occasion. I didn't know it at the time, but it was Bernard Hanna who told me how lucky I was!"

He was lucky because he made a good first impression on Sylvia and her family, and he would be rewarded with a positive response when he finally built up the nerve to ask her on a date. Bernard said to him: "I don't know how you came through 5th Street and carry Mr. Minns daughter out!"

The Beginning of Romance

At the time, Ephraim was 26 and Sylvia was 28. They were both at an age where marriage and settling down wouldn't have been a bad idea.

After his initial state of fright with carrying Sylvia lunch, he built up enough courage to ask her to have lunch with him in person. The next day, he picked her up at lunchtime.

They parked under a big fig tree behind a plaza in Palmdale that housed Canadian Imperial Bank, Modernistic Garden and Pet Supply, and other stores. Here, they had their first lunch together, and had a nice chat. Then he took her back to work.

Courting and First Date

For three weeks, Ephraim would call Sylvia and bring her lunch or take her to lunch. Since the vibes were feeling right, he built up the nerve to ask her out on a date. "I asked her if she wanted to go out on Friday, she said she wouldn't mind," Ephraim recalls. "Our first date was that Friday, and we went to King and Knights - that was the hottest spot in town at the time."

A Night to Remember

In 1973 the year of Independence, Bahamian entertainer King Eric formed the "King & Knights Club" - a venue that not only featured his band but a variety show that included carnival-style entertainment such as fire juggling and limbo dancing.

People came from all over the world to watch top Bahamian entertainers perform at King & Knights. Ephraim made sure that his first date with Sylvia would be one she would never forget.

An Ever-Deepening Bond

Ephraim said after three weeks of talking, he couldn't wait any longer to take her out. They had the time of their lives. "We danced and danced the night away," he said.

"When we left, we walked to the car and I opened the door. I stood at the door and as she approached I embraced her and kissed her on the cheek. I walked around to my side, reversed out of the parking lot, drove downtown and took her home."

"Before I dropped her off, I had to give her a kiss again... this time it wasn't on the cheek. You could just feel the goodness, the love, the care. It was just amazing."

Growing Closer

As the relationship progressed, everything was working out beautifully. "Her mom and I were talking like nobody's business," Ephraim said. "Her mother fell in love with me. One evening, she said to me, 'I have been inviting you to eat; you haven't eaten from us. You don't eat from people aye?'

"I used to always tell her that my mom had already cooked. I ate at home. It was taboo in our house to eat from people. "But I said to her, don't worry, the next time I come here I will eat; and I did." I sat at their dining room table and ate. It was Sylvia and I, her mothers, and one of her sisters. The food was very good." Sylvia's mom was never satisfied until I agreed to come back the next day and eat again."

A Future Together

Ephraim even managed to form a good relationship with Mr. Minns: "I always saw dad when I was there. He was a political fellow, so it was right up our alley and we would talk politics."

Ephraim knew he had found his future wife.

Chapter 5

The Engagement and Wedding

Family Approval

"MY PARENTS KNEW THAT I was serious about Sylvia, and they loved her," Ephraim said. "I remember I was home this Saturday. I was lying down on the sofa (called a settee back then). I was relaxing before it was time for me to head out to play a game of field hockey at Haynes Oval.

The phone rang. A young lady asked for me. My mother asked, 'Is this Sylvia?' The caller said, 'No'. My mother said to the young lady, 'Did Ephraim tell you he is engaged to a girl named Sylvia? Don't call this house anymore! He is engaged to Sylvia and that's it!" The funny thing is, Ephraim was not officially engaged as yet.

Setting the Stage for Union

"My parents were anxious to meet Sylvia's parents," he said. "I arranged a Sunday lunch at my parent's home, where I lived at that time."

It was a Sunday afternoon. The Jones Family attended Zion Baptist Church and the Minns family attended Transfiguration Baptist Church - both of these churches are of great historical and spiritual significance in The Bahamas.

After church, James and Violet Minns, along with their daughter Sylvia and her daughter Bunny, took up the invitation for Sunday dinner at the home of Alpheus and Alice Jones. This was just over a year after Ephraim and Sylvia first met.

A Joyous Engagement and Planning the Wedding

The pair got engaged during this Sunday dinner which went very well. Prior to the announcement, both families had the opportunity to converse, and asked the questions they wanted to ask.

Both fathers hit it off, and both mothers hit it off - something that remained the case throughout their lives. In fact, both Ephraim and Sylvia's parents remained towers of support throughout their lives, helping to make their marriage as successful as it turned out to be.

The wedding was a special occasion for both families, and one that was the culmination of much excitement.

A Day to Remember: The Wedding

Ephraim and Sylvia were married at Zion Baptist Church, the oldest church in New Providence, by Reverend Charles Smith. The date was Saturday, August 6, 1977. "My birthday was August 7 and I didn't want to forget it," Ephraim admitted.

His groomsmen included Alexander Gibson and Irvin Lightborne. Ephraim and Alex grew up like brothers. Ephraim is the Godfather of Alex's eldest child. They attended Scouts together. Irvin was in Ephraim's Scout troop.

"He was a little older, when he joined the troop," Ephraim said. "He attended St. Augustine's College. I said to him, 'I hope you didn't come to disrupt!' He said, 'No sir, I will make you proud! Boy, did he make me proud! He always came to me when he needed someone to talk to.

In Scouts, Ephraim is affectionately known as "Skip". One day, Irvin came to him and told him that at his workplace, the people he worked for did not know how to treat people. They had him working hard and didn't like to pay. "I suggested that he start his own company, and I would help him out."

Irvin started a party service company. Ephraim assisted him with business licensing, and he allowed him to store his items at Ephraim's place. By that time, Ephraim had his own photo lab on Wulff Road.

Today, Irvin's party company Bahamia Rentals is one of the most successful businesses in town. Irvin was proud to stand as a groomsman in Ephraim's wedding. Sylvia's sisters Agnes and Maxine stood as her bridesmaids.

After the ceremony, the reception was held at the Emerald Beach Hotel. Two hundred people attended. Everyone pitched in to help pull off such a big wedding - the couple and their parents.

Rickey Wells, Ephraim's dear friend, served as the wedding photographer.

The Beginning of a Lifetime Together

Sylvia's father brought her down the aisle. "She saw me and she started to smile," Ephraim lovingly recalled. "I start smiling too. Tears were running down her eyes.

Her father presented her to me. I said to her, 'You're crying because you have to leave home, hey? She nudged me." They shared a chuckle even in that somber moment. That's the way Ephraim and Sylvia were. They were always saying things that made each other laugh. They got married two and a half years after the day they met.

"That was the official start of a lifetime of happiness," Ephraim said. "She was amazing."

Chapter 6

Loving Her in Health

The Foundation of Love

"WE HAD SOMETHING CALLED love," Ephraim said of his marriage to Sylvia. "We had three answers we gave each other to any question - 'yes', 'ok', and 'no problem'.

We didn't have a spot in our relationship where we ever said 'no' to each other... and we never said 'never'. And 'why' was a question we never brought into our relationship. You will never get anywhere with 'why'. These are the things that helped us get through life."

"Sylvia has never ever said 'no' to me. That's the loving and caring individual she was."

Resolving Differences Before Bedtime

Anything that came up was resolved before bedtime in the Jones home. Ephraim and Sylvia made it a point that none of them could spend the night on the sofa or the floor. They had to come together and talk, and sleep together in the same bed every night.

"My wife was the boss of our home," he said. "Fellas would say, 'How in the world could you have your wife as the boss?' I said, because I am the CEO! She can't do anything without me that is over my budget!"

As the boss, she managed the house. I only dealt with matters she requested my assistance on as the CEO.

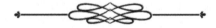

Building a Home Together

Ephraim and Sylvia were both striving young people. As newlyweds, both of them had their own properties and were building homes on them.

Sylvia's house was completed first, and they moved into her home in Golden Gates #1 after the wedding.

Ephraim's home, still under construction, was located on Poitier Avenue, Boyd Subdivision, which is the family home to this day.

Ephraim's father was adamant that Ephraim should complete his home and get his new bride under his roof as soon as possible.

Creating a Family Life

Ephraim adopted Sylvia's daughter, Bunny, and her last name was officially changed to Jones. Prior to this, she was carrying the Minns name. She did not have a relationship with her biological father. Ephraim wanted to make sure Bunny knew that she was important in his life, and that he was dedicated to raising her with love and care. Ephraim met Sylvia when Bunny was four years old. Right after Bunny's 6th birthday party at Sea Floor Aquarium in Chippingham, he told Sylvia that he would give Bunny his last name - she would become a Jones.

Ephraim and Sylvia provided Bunny with a good education, sending her to Xavier's Lower School, then St. Augustine's College, then College of The Bahamas, and then Belmont Abbey College, Charlotte, North Carolina.

After adopting Bunny as his own, Ephraim and Sylvia went on to bring two beautiful baby boys into the world. Ja-Ronn and Jamal would fill their lives with all the love and laughter they could stand. "My boys believe they own me," Ephraim says of them to this day.

All of the Jones children attended Xavier's. Mrs. Annabell Dean was the Principal at the time that Bunny went there. Mrs. Irma Iris Sandilands, a wonderful neighbour, took good care of the Jones children at Xavier's, and was instrumental in their academic success as they attended her evening classes, and she refused to accept any payment.

Ephraim's Entrepreneurial Venture

He did everything for Sylvia and the children. He was now an entrepreneur, so he had to be responsible for running his own business.

Ephraim had a photography concession store in a hotel. He is thankful for the assistance rendered to him by the father of the Bahamian nation, former Prime Minister, the late Sir Lynden Oscar Pindling, and former Progressive Liberal Party Chairman

Andrew "Dud" Maynard.

They were instrumental in securing him the spot in the hotel, which he, in turn, made into a thriving business.

A Life of Love and Commitment

"This was back in those days when you had one car. I would go back home at 7 am and drop Bunny and the boys to school. Bunny was at St. Augustine's College and the boys were at Xavier's (both Catholic Schools, as their mother had graduated from Aquinas College - a Catholic School). Then, I would drop Sylvia to work and go back to the store. At 12.45 pm, I would leave for lunch and pick up my wife. We went for lunch every day."

Cherishing Every Moment Together

"When I dropped her to work, I would kiss her. When I picked her up for lunch, I would kiss her. When I dropped her back to work, I would kiss her. And when I picked her up from work in the evenings, I would kiss her again." "Once they were all home, I would leave to go back to work around 6:30. Syl would say, 'What time are you coming home?' I would say, 'Give me about an hour.' Before I left home I would kiss her.

When I got home, she would be up and the minute I walked through the door, we would embrace and she would get another kiss." "She would ask me if I was going to take a shower first or if I was ready for dinner. We would always eat dinner together.

No matter what time I came home, even if I had a late-night at the hotel and I came home at 1 am, Sylvia would be waiting for me, and we would sit and eat dinner together."

"Sometimes, she would call me and say, 'I feel like eating Bamboo Shack tonight. Come for me.' I would go home and get her, and we would go to Bamboo Shack and get a chicken breast snack and share it."

Reflecting on Love and Marriage

"It was just an amazing relationship we had. Before we go to bed, that would be another five or six kisses. We just always had a kissing session going on."

"One of the biggest issues we have in this society is that people don't share love. Too often, we are missing out on so much. Too often today, women expect a lot from their man, but they don't give back. My wife never said no to me in our 44 years of being together. She made it a point to love me beyond measure, and I gave it back to her totally."

Chapter 7

The Love of Family

The Cornerstones of Marriage: Love and Responsibility

"SYLVIA'S JOB WAS TO take care of the home; my job was to provide," Ephraim said. "She would do homework with the kids. She was an accountant and a math enthusiast. She was amazing with numbers."

"I was one of those husbands who didn't know what the light bill and school fee was. Nothing in our home said 'You pay for this or I pay for that.' "I made provision and Sylv took care and managed our affairs."

'Between what we earned and our Asue (ancient African practice of group savings) we did it. She was an amazing individual."

Family Adventures and Vacations

"We went on vacation every year and we would take not only the children, but their friends as well."

Our boys were friends with Robert Sands' boys Delano and Omar - they loved to be with us. Bunny would bring her friend Bridgette along. I would always take my parents."

"We went on a cruise every year. I played field hockey and coached the ladies team. When we went to Washington to play, the whole family went. We had a game in Mandeville, Jamaica, and Syl went with us. One of her sisters, Maxine, was on the team."

Building a Family-Centered Life

"Syl and I were very family-oriented," Ephraim continued. "If you invited us to your house on a Sunday and children are not allowed, we are not going to come. We didn't go anywhere without the children."

It took Ephraim about three years from the time Sylvia moved into the home he built on Roland and Poitier Avenue for him to really finish everything in the home.

"When my father died, he left everything for me," he said. "I gave it to our older son. He ended up moving to Freeport, and then to the United States. So I finished building it for my son Jamal."

Education and Faith in the Family

The Joneses did their best to give their children a high-quality level of education. Ja-Ronn and Jamal graduated from St. Anne's High School and Bunny graduated from St. Augustine's - both private schools in Nassau, Bahamas.

All three of them went on to be educated at Belmont Abbey College, in the United States.

Sylvia, during her time at Aquinas College, had the opportunity to be taught by nuns, who impacted her greatly. Sylvia had a talent for sewing and math, and the nuns adored her, and she formed a great relationship with them.

Sylvia's Spiritual Journey and Influence

Even though her bedrock was Transfiguration Baptist Church, as an adult, Sylvia became a Catholic.

However, when she got married, her father advised her to follow her husband, and she attended Zion Baptist with her husband regularly.

She was willing to follow Ephraim to the moon and back.

A Life Designed by God

"My mother loved Syl so much that she never had to cook while my mother was alive," Ephraim said. "She chose to cook. My mother made it a point for Syl to have a good life.

"She would call Syl and say, 'I did some peas soup, come for it!' Come for this and come for that. Mom had her spoiled. We had a life designed by God. It was amazing how we lived."

Moments of Love and Sharing

"We had differences of opinion, but we never had fights and arguments." "Sometimes when she would call me at the hotel, the chef would ask her what she wanted to eat. She could put in her order and the chef would make a meal just for her, and I would take it home for her."

"My wife used to make about 200 rum cakes every Christmas," Ephraim shared, noting that her cakes were so good, she always had lots of orders at that time of year.

A Home Filled with Love and Hospitality

Sylvia was loved by many. She had a warm personality and she loved to share whatever she had, and she wanted to help everyone she could.

Every Sunday at the Jones household, Sylvia would cook for about 30 people. Their house was filled with friends and family who gathered to share her delicious meals. They ate to their heart's content, then turned around and took a plate home, because there was enough food for all.

Special Memories and Shared Laughter

At Christmas time, there were even more people at the Jones home. There would be about 50 people gathered for Christmas dinner - black and white people enjoying the Jones family dinner.

"Syl cooked everything herself," Ephraim said. "She never wanted any help from anyone in the kitchen.

If it was a big event, then my mom would come and give her a hand. Her mom was just as loving. You would think her mom only had one son-in-law!"

Treasured Moments and Lasting Memories

"I had so many memorable moments with Syl," he continued. "I remember one time we had some friends visiting from the United States. We took them up to Harbour Island for the day.

She was just beautiful. I said to her, 'You look sweet, juicy and delicious!' She was blushing. I said, 'Stop blushing!' And she laughed."

"That was such a special day, and the moment she laughed was caught on camera. It's one of my treasured photos of her."

Chapter 8

Loving Her in Sickness

The Onset of Sylvia's Illness

I N 2013, SYLVIA STARTED having some nagging pains in her legs, back, and waist. Each day, the pain seemed to grow worse.

"We went to the hospital, the Walk-in Clinic... no one seemed able to say what was happening," Ephraim recalls. "One doctor at the Walk-in Clinic gave Syl some medication. A few days later, the pain had gotten worse.

We went back to the Walk-in Clinic, and the same doctor advised us to get another opinion. It had gotten so bad that Syl needed help walking. She couldn't stand without having to lean, and she would have plenty of trouble to bend or to get into the bed."

Seeking Help and Hope

"I started inquiring about a wheelchair and a walker. We were very fortunate that the director of the Bahamas Red Cross, Mrs. Caroline Turnquest, gave us a wheelchair and Camile Fields gave us a walker with a chair so she could sit whenever she got tired."

"As time went by, we saw that nothing was working. We tried a massage therapist. We tried acupuncture. We would go into the sea so she could exercise in the salt water. Some days she had all the trouble in the world to walk. At this point, I had to wheel my wife around and she would feel pain at the slightest bump or shake. The pain was just unbearable."

A Sudden Turn

"At times she would cry out in pain. It was not easy to see a wife who was always vibrant and strong, constantly grimacing in pain." "One Sunday, I was getting ready for church and I fixed her breakfast. She told me that she didn't feel good. I told her that I wouldn't go to church, let's go to the doctor. She said, 'No, you go to church.' I went, then came back home and I fixed our lunch."

"Before I went to church that morning, she was standing up at one point when all of a sudden, her knees gave in. She fell, and as she fell, it seemed as if something just eased her down between where I was standing and the chair. I didn't get there in time to catch her, but it was as if an inflated cushion eased her to the ground as she fell.

The Lord was in the bedroom that morning, the way she fell without nothing being bruised or broken. I called our son Jamal to help. The way her legs were, I thought they were broken at first; but nothing was wrong with her. She still told me to go to church, and if she felt bad when I returned, we would go to the doctor."

A Visit to the Hospital

"We ate our Sunday lunch when I returned. By that evening, I told her that she didn't look good, and we should go to the doctor. She said, 'Ok'. For her to say 'Ok', I knew it was a problem, because she doesn't like going to the doctor."

"We went to Doctor's Hospital that evening and they ran tests. They checked her out, and very late that evening, they decided to put her on the ward. About 3:30/4:00 am, Jamal and I left Doctor's Hospital to head home."

"The hospital was keeping her in and the doctor wanted to run tests. We collected some items for her from home, and we returned to the hospital after 5 am. When we returned, I asked to speak to the doctor. I said to the doctor, 'Tell me something, do you think she has cancer?' The doctor said, 'I am having the specialist have a look at her in the morning'. He said the specialist would be able to help me out tomorrow."

Diagnosis and Determination

"I didn't sleep that night. By 10 am, I was back at the hospital. I went to see her and she had that beautiful smile as usual. She said she was ok, and that she slept well. I waited on the doctor. When he came, he said they would run tests and so on. That's when we found out that she was in a little bit of trouble."

Sylvia was diagnosed with myeloma - a cancer of the plasma cells. Ninety-five percent of her body was covered with this nuisance called cancer. "I began saying in my head, 'Why are you in my wife's body? What are you doing in her life?' Then I paused and said to myself, 'Whatever the Lord does is well done'. His purpose and will must be done."

"I went back into the room. She was so upbeat in spite of the pain... What a woman! After a few days, Syl was allowed to go home. She was still in pain but she was happy she was going home." She started doing chemotherapy with Dr. Theodore Turnquest. She was such a determined woman - determined to beat this cancer.

The Struggle with Pain and Love

"The pain was so harsh at times, that the smile that was so readily available was gone - it just wasn't there." "I watched my wife drop several dress sizes."

"Many days I cried. Many nights I cried. She never knew. I never let her see me crying. I always made sure she never saw me crying. I was that strong." "I was a husband who was there for his wife. It was not easy seeing someone you love not able to do anything for herself - absolutely nothing. Imagine a woman who always found time to do something - from sewing to cooking - to baking.

She was so active and full of life. She was a caring wife and mother. A sincere, dedicated woman who loved God." "Wow, what a woman!" "I just had to have a conversation with our God daily. I asked the Lord to bring my wife Sylvia back to life.

I said, 'She is one of your children who can honestly speak about your goodness and kindness to her, and especially your healing powers'. 'Here is a woman who can really be a testimony to your grace and mercies'.

Now, it was my time to give my wife our wedding vows' commitment." "We vowed to love each other in sickness and in health. Was the Lord testing my vows by giving Syl this pain?"

Ephraim's Devotion and Care

Syl started to spend more time in bed because of the pain. Whenever it was time to move her, Ephraim faced a big challenge. He became her nurse, and he would have to find a way to make his wife as comfortable as possible.

When making up the bed, Ephraim would have to put the blue hospital pads on the bed, then put a layer of plastic on the bed. He would then place two large towels on the bed, and another layer of blue hospital pads.

Ephraim would then lovingly bathe his wife like a baby. Once that was done, the tough part came - time to get her back in the bed. She was not able to turn her body by herself.

Five to six times a night, Ephraim would have to turn his wife's body for her so she could be comfortable. Sometimes by the third turn, his wife would be soaked with sweat from head to toe. He would have to pull the plastic and the towels over to his side of the bed, then clean her up and put on a fresh set of clothes.

"I don't know if husbands and wives really know the meaning of their wedding vows when they say in sickness and in health," Ephraim said. "I had to put Depends diapers on my wife for more than a year. I would go to work, spend about two hours, then head back home.

My wife would tell me sometimes that she felt like eating a particular thing. I would take my time and fix it for her. By the time she got the food, her taste for it was gone. This is where patience comes in.

"Sometimes when I would get Syl ready for bed, she would squeeze my hand. I would ask, 'Syl, are you trying to say something to me?' She would break a smile. You know smiles were so rare at this point."

Chapter 9

A Testament of Love

The Rigorous Routine of Treatment

"THE FIRST FEW MONTHS of treatment by Dr. Turnquest were so interesting. If she had to be at her doctor's appointment by 9:30 or 10 am, we would have to start preparing from 5:30 am."

"First, I would prepare myself to get Syl ready. We would say our morning prayers. Then it was time to get her ready. We would start with me putting my arms under her neck. Then to raise her, I would put one pillow under her, then a second, a third, a fourth, and a fifth pillow - all to raise her up.

As I am lifting her, she would moan in pain. Then, with my arms still around her, I would pull the wheelchair close to the bed. I had to pause a while because she didn't have any body balance. I had to be careful with her. Any fall and something could break."

Assisting with Daily Activities

"Once I got the wheelchair close to the bed, I would put both of her arms around my neck so they wouldn't hang and make the pain worse. As I lifted her out of the bed, I would ease her into the wheelchair and take her to the bathroom. I have to be so careful because if there was any bump or shake she would scream in pain."

"I had to get the water temperature just right. Then I would lift her, one leg at a time, into the shower to sit on the shower chair. There was a window sill, and she would rest her hand on it. She couldn't take the shower water directly on her; it was too painful. So, I would use a plastic basin to bathe her. I would pour the water over her gently, then soap her body and rinse her. Syl couldn't even raise her hands. It was so painful."

Reflecting on Commitment and Care

"Can you imagine, after 37 years of marriage, that this was my first exam on commitment, love, appreciation, and care?" "Some nights I came home and prepared my wife Syl for bed. I would feed her, bathe her, then put her to bed. The minute I put my head on the pillow, I am out like a lamp.

Sometimes, she would try to reach for things on the nightstand. She didn't want to wake me. Sometimes the item would drop. I would get up and say, 'Syl, why didn't you wake me?' She didn't want to wake me. I told her even if I am sleeping, please wake me up for whatever she needs.

But what could you expect? She was a replica of my mother, Alice Jones, and her mother, Violet Minns - two women who held their pain close to their hearts (so the world would not know) and they were both so independent."

Family Support and Friendship

Sometimes, Jamal would start making breakfast for the family when he heard his parents get up. He and Ja-Ronn, whenever he was in town, would assist their father in taking care of their mother. They would cook for her, they bathed her, and they washed her soiled clothes daily.

Sometimes, their mother could not control her bowels, but they never stopped assisting with cleaning her and her bedroom, ensuring that she was as comfortable as possible.

"I would brush her hair up and put her clip in it," Ephraim shared. "I would frill her hair out to the back the way she liked, and sometimes, I would put a little powder on her face for her. I dressed her, cleaned her, bathed her, cooked for her - the works."

Sylvia's friends were also a great help, including Lorraine Mullings, Sonia Hamilton, Joy Khan, Shirley Smith, Barbara Holder, and Janet Styles. Ephraim said Sylvia's friends were 'unbelievable'. They came every week to spend time with her and to clean the house for her. There was nothing they wouldn't do for her.

Her brother Arthur was also an amazing help to her. He would come and assist us, and he would lift her and put her in our vehicle for her doctor's appointment. He loved his sister; he was faithful and came every morning when she had a doctor's appointment.

A Courageous Battle with Cancer

Sylvia endured this most difficult phase for about five months before the chemotherapy started to work just enough for her to be a little more mobile. She had to have a bone marrow transplant, and she and Ephraim began traveling abroad for additional medical care. She was taken to Cleveland Clinic in Florida. They confirmed the diagnosis of myeloma cancer that the Bahamian doctors gave us.

Ephraim said they did a wonderful job at Cleveland Clinic, Sylvia was continuing chemotherapy, and they were getting some positive results.

Ja-Ronn's wife was a big support and help whenever we traveled to Florida. When in Nassau, Kim Wilson was a tremendous help to Syl. "With all this love surrounding her," Ephraim said, "We could ask for nothing more."

Embracing Joy Despite the Pain

Prior to all of this, their son Ja-Ronn had planned a cruise for them that was to take place in 2014. Sylvia told the doctor that her son had a cruise planned for them. She said jokingly, that she was going on that trip, even if she had to crawl. She told the doctor that there was no way she was missing the trip, and whatever happened to her after that, she would be ok with it.

Ja-Ronn purchased a motorized wheelchair for his mother, and the trip was set.

Ephraim recalls a happy time: "We went on that trip and we had the time of our lives! She defied all odds and we went away. She was in pain most days, but that didn't keep her from moving. She did everything she could to have fun on that trip. The only thing she didn't do was dance!

The family trip was important for the Jones. Family is everything to them. Bunny, Jamal and Ja-Ronn grew up with them going to church as a family together every Sunday. They would have lunch together as a family.

Sylvia loved Ephraim so much that she got to learn every sport that he liked, just so she could sit with him and watch the games. "I liked to watch field hockey, which I played, and we also watched softball, baseball, football, and basketball. She sat with me and watched all the games, and she was never a nuisance.

We used to have Superbowl parties at the hotel, and eventually, we started having them at home, and Sylvia would host them."

So, that cruise time was important family time, and an opportunity for them to connect and feel close the way they did before the boys became men and before Sylvia fell ill. She had so much fun through the pain, that a photograph captured of her showed a woman full of joy, so much so that it did not seem like the same woman who was suffering from myeloma.

After that cruise of a lifetime, she continued to receive chemotherapy treatments.

Enduring Love Amidst the Challenge

Sylvia fought to have a successful bone marrow transplant. She had to eat lots of ice to keep the sores out of her mouth. She was successful as she never developed the sores.

Doctors removed her marrow, cleaned it, and put it back, Ephraim said. "One day, I went into her room, and she didn't know I was coming," he said. "They were prepping her. I went to the room and stood at the door and she was struggling to get out of the bed. All the drips and what not were on her."

"She held her head up and saw me at the door. You should have seen that smile. She smiled like it was Christmas and everything she wanted in her world was there. I went over and hugged her and kissed her."

Chapter 10

A New Lease on Life

A New Beginning

A FTER A SUCCESSFUL BONE marrow transplant, the medical staff at Miami University Hospital told Sylvia she had a new lease on life.

It was a big surprise when the staff walked through the door of Sylvia's room with a birthday cake and balloons. They told her that she was starting all over again, and this was her first birthday!

With this new lease on life, Sylvia returned to some of her normal activities, such as cooking and caring for her loved ones. She was especially happy to be able to have the strength to spend time with her grandchildren. By this time, Bunny had 4 children; Ja-Ronn had 3 and has since welcomed his 4th child into the world; and Jamal has 1.

Cherished Family Moments

"She was still an active grandma," Ephraim recalled. "She and Ria were close. She taught Juliana to sneak her chips and sweets. Julianna would go to her grandmother's secret spot and bring all the treats to me.

Aidan and Jia - were so loving to their grandma. Rhylee was the talker, and she and Syl would sit and they would be talking away.""

"Things were back to just about normal. It was like she had a new lease on life. It didn't take much for her to be back to normal. She never one day complained about anything.

People would say, 'Man you don't look sick!' She was always prepared to share her experience with persons who were going through the same thing. She was just an amazing individual."

"We would go for drives and sit on the beach. We would go to Florida to shop. Her friend Jan in Florida would pick Syl up from the airport and take her anywhere she wanted to go. What a blessing Jan was to us."

Facing Challenges Again

Sylvia did not take sick again until July of 2021. By November of that year, Ephraim had to start assisting her with bathing again. "The pain got more severe and everything started collapsing on her. I think she never fully got rid of the pain."

"It was rough, but we had insurance, and that helped tremendously. The Lord takes care of his own.

Because Sylvia managed our affairs, we always had something extra somewhere. I never had to pay any bills. I made sure she had money every week when I was working."

A Love Like No Other

"It was just amazing to see someone sick, more worried about me than herself. Whatever she had she would share with me even before she touched it. Even when she was feeling bad, she would still say, 'Eph, I will go with you'. And she would drive with me.

She was always more concerned if I was hurting than if she was. Her life was centered around me and the children."

"I have never seen an individual love someone the way my wife loved me. I had to give her, at all times, a special kind of love.

She took care of our home very well. Our children got a proper education. She would argue with them if they got a 'B' on their report card. I would look at her and think, 'What a woman'! She was a strong drill sergeant that took good care of the home."

Reflections on a Blessed Union

"My wife was so inviting that I kissed her so many times a day. We would go to Florida and she would tell Ja-Ronn to get special things for me. On Sundays when we had guests, no one would eat until she got home.

We had a wonderful marriage. Violet and James Minns were my inspiration. My mother must have taught my wife how to take care of me. Her mother Violet taught her daughter how to treat her husband.

Alfred and Alice Jones brought up their children in a way that was second to none. "They taught me how to love, and I poured that into my family."

"In life, sometimes when we look back and we realize our blessing. The Lord created a certain individual just for you."

Chapter 11

Reflecting on Sylvia's Strength

"WATCHING A GOOD WIFE... an excellent wife... become sick, (Ephraim shakes his head......after being with this woman for 44 years... looking at her, and there is nothing I can do to help her anymore...)," Ephraim shared, reflecting on one of the most difficult times of his life. But even in this difficult time, Sylvia was still beautiful. She was still graceful. She was still smiling as best she could. She was still gracious and thankful for the help, the love, and the support of others.

"When she would see me, she would light up, even though she was sick in hospital," Ephraim recalled. "Most of the time, I was feeling her pain. When I would say to her, Syl, something isn't right, she would say that she is ok." "What an amazing woman! You know she is hurting, yet she is still trying her best to smile because she knows her husband is feeling the same pain she is feeling."

"Sickness is not an easy road. If any of you are going through this difficult period called sickness, when your other half can't do anything for themselves and you are there, I know that it's not an easy road." "The strength that I had, I just wanted to know how I could give that to her. No matter what I did for her at that time, the pain was still there."

Love in Times of Sickness

"I watched her so many times just staring... because of the painkillers she had... she was just staring. But it was such a beautiful stare as she lay there." "Sometimes, tears just came to my eyes as I watched her. But I always took pride and joy in being able to sit with her every day when she was in hospital.

Whether it was at the University of Miami where she had her bone marrow transplant, or Cleveland Clinic where she got the rest of her care while in America, I would spend the whole day with her from morning until night."

"I would say to anyone who has to go through this experience with their spouse - genuine love is so important at this time. I saw where the love that Syl and I shared helped her so much. And the peacefulness of her time during her sickness helped me so much."

"She was so comfortable and so peaceful. When you looked at her, you never saw a grimacing face. It was like hey, is she really sick? But we knew that her inside was deteriorating because of the weakening of the bones."

Gratitude for Family Support

"I want to say a special thanks to my sons for all they did for their mother. When you watch your children help you bathe their mother, and knowing that when you are not there, they are bathing her... they are simply amazing."

"We had such a beautiful life with Syl. Every Sunday, we would attend Zion Baptist Church. Before church, we would have our own morning devotions at home. We would pick a chapter of the Bible, and everyone would have a couple of verses to read. After church, we would have lunch with my parents, and spend the evening with her parents."

A Life of Love and Sacrifice

Ephraim found so many ways to show love and self-sacrifice with his family. When it was time for lunch, he would invite Sylvia to take up her food first. Then, Bunny would take up hers, followed by Ja-Ronn and then Jamal. "In this way, he taught his son to have respect for his elder siblings and respect the laws of the family."

As Ephraim reflected on this wonderful life, he gave thanks for being blessed abundantly. Even though the sickness of his wife was hard, loving her was still easy. "I think I saw my wife cry once," he said. "Her friends told me that she cried, but I only saw her cry once."

Peaceful Transition

In the days before she died, Sylvia was so angelic... so peaceful. "The day before she left us, I held my wife and I prayed to the Lord. At this point, she wasn't responding anymore. I said to the Lord: 'Lord, if you are ready to take her, I will be at peace with it'. The next day, we visited Syl at the hospital. Ja-Ronn dropped me off at the airport and returned to be with his mother. By the time I landed in Nassau, Ja-Ronn called to say she left us." "It's not the end of the world when a loved one is missing from your life. It's rough and difficult, but remember, it's not the end of the world."

Chapter 12

The Love of Friends

E PHRAIM AND SYLVIA'S FRIENDS absolutely love them. One by one, their closest friends reveal their love and respect.

Rev'd Canon Stephen E. R. Davies

JaRonn... "Hey, dad what size suit do you wear?"

Dad... "You better ask ya Ma 'cause I don't know."

Now that exchange which happened the weekend of 5th February tells a lot about who Syl was especially when it came to her Ephraim and her family.

I met Ephraim 51 years ago. I was 9 years old and he was the 18-year-old Leader of the 8th Bahamas Boys Scout Troop. Ephraim or 'Skip' as we called him was a rugged and tough task master who tolerated no bologna from the boys or their parents especially those who wanted to tell him how to run things. It was his way or the highway.

It was about 5yrs later Skip started to become a gentler, but still firm personality, you see he had met Syl, and he was a changed man. He couldn't wait for parents to collect their boys on a Friday night so he could see his Syl.

Syl quickly became a part of the troop activities. Cook-outs to raise money for summer camps, here at home or abroad. Syl baked macaroni and other goodies for our Sunday Family Day when we camped at Adelaide. Syl traveled with our Troop to Atlanta and Mexico, Bunny too... yes Ephraim didn't leave her behind.

For some strange reason, Skip thought I was his special project, which he took to heart, and I will leave him to tell that story. Skip started to tell people I was his oldest child and of course, if I was Skip's child Syl was my other mother and she treated me and my family with that special love and care that is uniquely Syl.

Those who knew her, know of what I speak. Syl was not perfect, you can't tell Skip that, but Syl was real people, she was genuine and she was pure in sharing herself with others.

You would think listening to Skip that he was the boss in the house, but the truth is Syl was the quiet storm behind the throne, she knew how to support her man and make him the king he always wanted to be and is still trying to be today.

Syl took care of her home and family, and her kitchen was always turning out mouth-watering delights, even when she was not in the best of health. I believe that's why Jamal is becoming a chef in his own right.

Syl enjoyed opening her home to friends and feeding them like they didn't eat otherwise. Syl didn't have a sweet tooth but she gave all her friends sweet teeth, with fruit cake, carrot cake, banana bread, and the like.

You could never find Skip between 1-2 pm in the day, because he was having lunch with Syl; that was sacred time and space. I think it's easier to count the days they did not have lunch than to count the days they were together. Some of us could learn something from that.

Skip I can't know or feel your pain, I think I can relate to Bunny, Ja-Ronn, and Jamal because I lost my good father in July 2021. I will miss Syl too.

On behalf of my family, my Mom and siblings, and the Boys of the 8th Bahamas Boys Scouts who have now become men, and are still proud to call you Skip; I commend Syl to our Good Gracious and merciful God, to keep her safe until we meet again.

May her soul and the souls of the faithful departed rest in peace.

Amen.

Janet Styles

I shall always miss my dear friend and sister, Syl. She made me laugh and she was always there to help me figure out things.

I first met Syl through my niece Shirley who worked with Syl at Royal Bank for many years and were close friends.

Syl was fearless and forever curious about everything. She was a devoted wife to her loving husband, Eph, and a loving mother to her precious sons, Ja-Ronn and Jamal. And three beautiful grandchildren.

She was a mighty force to be reckoned with. Syl was a gift to the world. She made it better. She fought cancer for many years and we became even closer during these final years, and I'm forever thankful for that time. I love you dearly MAMA!

Mona M. Culmer

Syl and I worked at the Royal Bank of Canada for many years. We became closer after she learned that I was in Ft. Lauderdale taking chemotherapy. After, I would travel twice a year to the doctor. During those trips, I would pick up Syl and we would go shopping, etc.

Syl had an eye for fashion. She was a human GPS. She knew Ft. Lauderdale like the back of her hand. Syl loved to cook and bake. She would always have a delicious Bahamian meal and a slice of cake for me.

Syl was so strong. She didn't complain. That is what I have learned from her. To this day, I move around like Syl, if you didn't know the facts, you would not know there is a problem.

My trips used to be a mini vacation, knowing that I was going to meet up with Syl but now they are, 'just going to the doctor trips.'

Missing you Syl!

Geneva Aranha

As a student in St. Cecilia's Primary School heading to mass at 7 am on weekdays, our path (Syl and I) would meet most mornings as she would be walking to Aquinas College. We would always greet each other with a smile and good morning. Upon my graduation from Aquinas, fate had it I joined the Royal Bank of Canada and after several years, Syl was transferred to the branch I was at, and our friendship developed.

I always admired her and Ephraim's happiness as husband and wife. Five days when he dropped and picked her up from work they greeted each other with a kiss and had lunch together every day when possible. Syl loved her God, husband, family, and even her friends. Ephraim's parents, especially his mom, treated her as her biological child and Syl always spoke about her.

Syl was a beautiful person inside and outside. Having a heart of gold, she gave unselfishly to others without you having to ask. I miss my morning chats with her. Syl, take your rest as you are truly missed.

Alexander Gibson

E P H R A I M

E - Excellent

P - Patient

H - Humble

R - Resourceful

A - Ambitious

I - Impressive

M - Marvelous

My friend for over fifty years and counting.

A man for all seasons!

Shirley Smith

How best can I describe a friend who meant so much to me? I could call her a confidante, an advisor, a kindred spirit because we shared so much in common, or simply irreplaceable because that is what Syl was to her family and friends.

To her family, Syl was a rock, a source of faith, hope, and love all rolled into one. She often spoke of her undying and unconditional love for Ephraim, her children, and her grandchildren. She was not only a mother to her children but to all who knew her. Syl remained hopeful even as her health deteriorated. She nor Ephraim had time for self-pity and doubt, and he would often caution me if he saw me show any signs of it. I can say without a doubt that I didn't have the strength Syl had nor her faith for that matter; it was unshakeable.

To her co-workers, Syl was respected and admired. I think we were 'Royal Bank rebels' because we were both unafraid to speak our minds and stand up for what we believed to be right. Syl was fearless and stubborn and performed her job and carried out her duties with excellence. So well in fact, that very few people could think to walk in her shoes. Syl was dedicated to her work but drew the line when it came to her family. Nothing came before Ephraim and her children and when Royal Bank decided to test that, they would no doubt fail.

To me, Syl was a forever friend, the one that comes into your life for a lifetime and not a reason or season. I could talk to her about anything. She was a good listener and always gave good advice. She had a smile and laugh that was infectious, and she made you a better person by just being around her.

I am so happy I introduced my Aunt Janet to Syl a few years ago. They immediately hit it off and were friends until the end. I warned Syl that Janet was a talker, especially about politics. Syl was forewarned though, not afraid, and the two developed a friendship consisting of spending many Saturdays together. Whenever I visited Florida, the three of us would do lunch, have pedicures, and of course, go shopping. I am so grateful for those precious memories.

Syl fought an eight-year battle with cancer, many years of treatment, pain, and suffering, yet she always remained positive and optimistic. She was determined to fight this illness and rarely complained, if at all. Even as the pain grew worse, she bore it, willing to endure just so she could spend more time with her family.

Thank you, Ephraim, Ja Ronn, and Jamal for your undying love and devotion to her care. You explored every avenue and every available treatment option in the hopes that something would work and eventually cure her.

Ephraim, I know how much you adored and loved Syl. Continue with her special family traditions. Continue to speak to and about her. Talk to the children and grandchildren and all the friends reminiscing about stories about her. Her beautiful spirit will surely live on in all those whose lives she touched. She was such a kind and generous person that even the medical professionals and staff of the Cleveland Clinic loved her, and she loved right back with the treats that she baked and took for them.

As her friend, I am grateful to them and all family and friends who supported and prayed for her.

I visited Syl the day before she went back to Florida for what would be the last time. We spent several hours together and spoke about so many things including the loves in her life Ephraim and the children, our RBC days, and the injustices we endured there. There was nothing off limits and I am grateful for that time together. Her pain is finally over but as she lays peacefully, I know her spirit will always be present among us. Her amazing qualities will remain in our hearts that will be heavy, and filled with so many memories. I will miss you my friend, but it's time for you to take your eternal rest in peace that you are so deserving of after a battle so well and bravely fought. I am proud to have been your friend.

P.S. I dreamt about Syl recently.... she was in a garden. She wore a beautiful long white dress. Her black hair was streaked with gray. She gave me a big box with smaller white gift-wrapped boxes inside. She instructed me to give them to everyone. Each box was labeled: Ephraim, Ja-Ronn, Jamal, Kelly, and all her family and friends, most of whom I recognized. I believe that she, in typical Syl fashion is concerned about each one of you. I would like to think that the boxes contained personal messages and wanting you to know and be comforted that she is happy and is finally at peace.

Sonia Cox-Hamilton

Sylvia Minns-Jones has been my friend for over 50 years. I met her when I went to work at the Royal Bank of Canada Main Branch in 1967. We remained friends from then to the time of her passing. Sylvia was an extraordinary person in that she was frank, outspoken, and really quite the person you would want to back you up at any time; and I was likewise to her.

She was so swift in what she had to do with her hands. The first thing I remember her being so good with was sewing. We were young girls at Royal Bank. By that time, I had already been married and my children were born and I was to the point where I was moving to another chapter of my life. But Sylvia would, on the lunch hour, say, 'Let's go to GR Sweeting!' We would go and get material to make a dress or two and the only thing she needed me to do was sit with her and talk with her while she would cut those two dresses freehand, sit to that machine sewing, and we would be laughing and talking the whole time. In no time, we would have, by 7pm, two brand new dresses to go out in.

I remember those days with so much joy. She also was able to sew little girls' dresses. I had three, and she was so happy to do that for them.

After a while Sylvia, realizing my situation... an item that stands out in my mind is when I told her I needed to get out of a bad marriage. My husband was very aggressive. I had tried, several times to get him out of my life but it wasn't working. She went home and she told her father and her father, Mr. James Minns, a giant of a man that he was, said 'I could deal with that'. She said to me,

'Pack your things, my daddy coming'. I had everything I needed packed. He pulled up that day in his rickety old truck and he said, 'Gal, ya ready'? I said, 'Yes, sir'. I went into that truck feeling safe that no one could harm me as long as I was there with him. And that is how I got out of a really terrible situation.

Sylvia remained friends with me throughout her life. I am the godmother of her eldest daughter, Bianca Kelly Minns Jones Murphy, aka "Bunny". I am really the aunt of them all, from Bunny to Ja-Ronn to Jamal and even the grandchildren. I love them all.

She was a warrior, and all throughout her sickness, I never once heard Sylvia complain; I never once heard her saying she was tired; she just pushed on to the very end.

For that, she should be commended as a true hero. I miss her, I think of her all the time... I miss her laugh, I miss our talks, I miss her cooking, her baking, and her kind ways. Most of all, I miss having a friend to confide in and talk with. I shall keep her memory alive as long as I am alive and it is an honor for me to say in this lifetime, that she was my friend for life.

Lorraine Mullings

Nothing can replace the love of a sister/ friend. Syl you flew away but you are in my soul forever you'll stay. Syl you made the bad times good and the good times unforgettable. Your life was a blessing. Your memory will always remain in my heart Grateful for the time we shared together. Missing you every day.

Sharon Wallace

SYL

Our lives go on without you

But nothing will ever be the same

We have to hide our heartache

As tears continue to fall

At the mention of your name

You did so many things for so many people

Your heart was kind and true

And when we needed someone to talk to or something I knew I could depend on you

With love in my heart, your memories will forever live with us

Sleep on my friend and take your rest we loved you but jesus loved you best

Until we meet again on that beautiful shore where there is no more pain and suffering

Dr. Harold A. Munnings

Sylvia Jones appeared as I had imagined she would be when I first met her; an elegant woman. She was an attentive and gracious host at dinner. We had little interaction after that, for a long while, until cruel chance gave her a devastating illness. Over a stretch of years, the disease robbed her of her energy, then of her stature, and finally of her mobility. She endured agonizing back pains as the condition weakened and collapsed her spine. Through all this, she remained positive, loving, and grateful. I witnessed her outlook firsthand as her husband entrusted me with aspects of her care.

Tourists and other strangers could be forgiven for mistaking Ephraim Jones, Sylvia's husband as just a photographer. At the photo stand and at the wedding party, he cuts the stereotypical figure, with his camera in hand and friendly manner. But Ephraim is no ordinary photographer and his camera is a magician's misdirection.

In The Bahamas, Skip, as he is known to the tribe of men he helped to raise as a boy scout master, is more powerful than any official in the Office of the Prime Minister. He is more like a permanent secretary-at-large, without the title and the hangers-on.

Skip activated his contacts and flexed his influence in the service of Sylvia when she fell ill. The resources that he brought to bear eased her suffering and extended her life. As a member of his normally invisible entourage, I was able to spend more time with Sylvia during the final years of her life. I was touched and blessed by each interaction. She demonstrated the veracity of the saying; if you want to truly know someone's character, see how they handle adversity.

Chapter 13

Everlasting Legacy

Embracing Love and Togetherness

"WHAT SYL TAUGHT ME was something I grew up on. More love... love, love, love... togetherness, sharing." "We never had a money problem. We never had a money issue no matter how small the money was because Syl would have had a portion of my salary every week. I would have been left with about 20% of my salary which was for gas and other incidentals. Because she took care of the household."

Partnership in Marriage

"I have always shared with fellas who say, 'You keep saying that your wife is the boss of the house'. I say to them, yes, she is the boss. They would say, 'Come on man, ain't no woman supposed to be no boss of the house!' I say to them, that's why you guys continually get into trouble. I am the CEO! She runs the house. I am not there to see a lot of things that happen on a regular basis. She is there. She makes sure homework is done. She makes sure bills are paid. She makes sure school fees are paid, and grocery is there. She just did an amazing job in taking care of our house. I didn't have to worry. I didn't have to ask her one day, what happened to that $2 we had saved. I didn't have to do that. She was such an extraordinary woman."

The Joy of Family Vacations

"I made arrangements for our trip every year. We went on a cruise. We found out that the boys were eating too much. We had to stop going on regular vacations. We had to go on cruises so they could eat just about any time they wanted. When we traveled to the United States or anywhere else, they would have breakfast, and 15 minutes later, 'Dad, we're hungry!'

We had to find a way to get out of that. So we went on cruises and we found out, because of those cruises, our boys - and the whole family enjoyed themselves. We paid one set fee and we could do whatever activities we wanted, and the boys could each as much as they wanted"

The Foundation of Family Values

"So that family life that we had - the way Syl and I were brought up, we passed it on to them. You come across a woman who is totally committed to taking care of her family. I always tell young fellas who plan on getting married, 'Did you have a chance to look at the young lady's home? Did you look at it properly - not haphazardly?' Go in and see how she speaks to her mother; and how she treats her father. See how they live together.

My wife and her family - it was just unbelievable how they live. You could have seen the love, felt the love. My mother-in-law just taught them well. Her parents did what my parents did. My daddy never went to the food store. My daddy didn't go and pay the bills. He put that money there, and that was it. And if he got extra money, he would still put a little extra there again. Because in those days, my father bought numbers. He had all the dream books in the world. Thruppence, shilling... so he bought these numbers and whenever he would win extra money, he would make sure and give mom something. And you would hear him sometimes, 'I give Alice 'lil something, and she's still grumbling you know, because I didn't give her all!"

Laughter and Love in Family Life

"My boys used to come home and say to Syl, 'Mum, boy, dad, and mum had a good one today.' Syl would say, 'What happened'. Dad (their grandfather) would be sitting at the front room window, and when someone came to the gate, Pops would say to Mum in the kitchen, 'Alice, who is this out here?' And Alice would then say, 'Aren't you there sitting down, why don't you go and see who it is!' That's the type of arguments - if you want to call it arguments - that we had. These little funny jokes, that's all we had.

We never had these fighting and arguments, rowing, cussing, and carrying on because my parents never did it. I never heard my inlaws do it. So, my wife came into something that was parallel to what she was used to. The most noise would have been me running on with something. And I would say, Syl, you heard me? Sylvie, I am speaking to you. And she would say, "I didn't hear you'. And by that time, I would say ok, alright, don't bother with it, that's alright. I know you hear me. And that's how it was. We didn't have this running on and stuff."

Nurturing Children with Values

"If you look at my children, you would see that they were brought up a certain way and they lived that life. It wasn't a pretentious life. We had that type of relationship because of where my wife came from. She was always responsible for the home, and she did a wonderful job. The Lord truly blessed our family and we ensured that we brought up our children and grandchildren to be respectful and decent."

"

Planning and Sharing Life Together

"I planned our vacations. I always planned ahead of time and I would go ahead and arrange it. We went on a vacation every year.

Sometimes twice a year. Whenever we go on a cruise, my wife would say, 'Eph, I know you are going to the casino tonight, I put that there for you'. She would give me a hundred dollars every night we went on a cruise because she didn't have to pay for any vacation any time. And she just showed her love and appreciation."

A Testament of Unconditional Love

When the boat was in port, we would go shopping and she would say, 'Eph, come try this on, see if you like it'. I would say no, I don't like it Syl. And she would say, well I like it, and I am getting it, and that's it. We would go into the men's shop and Syl would say, 'You need another suit, Eph'. I would say no, I am ok. She would still buy a suit. She knew my size. She knew what she liked and what she wanted for me, and that was it." "She made it a point to purchase something special. The chain and bracelet I wear is something special she wanted me to have, despite me saying I didn't want anything. She still bought it. What a woman. Nothing was too good for her family."

The Blessing of a Life Partner

"She was a woman who made sure that she took care of every little detail, every little item. I didn't have to go shopping, because she did that. She was away, she was sick, and she would still buy me something. She would buy something for her brother Arthur. She would buy something for her brother Freddie. She would always buy something for her grandkids. So she was just extraordinary."

"She was a blessing that the Lord gave to me, and I was a blessing the Lord gave to her."

Chapter 14

Epilogue

As Ephraim reflects on his life with Sylvia, their enduring love and resilience is evident in every memory. Their journey, filled with both joy and challenges, is a powerful testament to the strength of the human spirit and its ability to find hope and light, even in the darkest times.

Their story, encompassing both the everyday moments and the significant milestones, highlights the profound impact of enduring love and mutual support, emphasizing the beauty and strength found in a life shared together.

The Essence of True Partnership

Ephraim and Sylvia's story is a testament to the essence of true partnership. It teaches us that a genuine relationship is built on mutual respect, understanding, and an unwavering commitment to support each other through every phase of life.

Their bond exemplifies how a partnership can flourish when rooted in love, shared values, and a deep sense of togetherness.

Navigating Life's Challenges with Grace

Their journey through Sylvia's illness highlights the importance of navigating life's challenges with grace and strength. Ephraim's dedication to Sylvia during her health struggles underscores the depth of their love and the importance of compassion and empathy in a relationship. It reminds us that in moments of vulnerability, the strength of our bonds is truly tested and proven.

Legacy of Family Values

The life they built together, centered around family, faith, and community, stands as a beacon of the enduring importance of these timeless values. Their story encourages us to cherish and nurture our family bonds, instill strong values in our children, and remain steadfast in our commitments to our loved ones.

Resilience in the Face of Adversity

Sylvia's bravery and resilience in the face of adversity, and Ephraim's unwavering support, offer an inspiring message of hope and courage. It shows us that with love, patience, and faith, it is possible to face life's toughest challenges while maintaining dignity and grace.

An Everlasting Impression

In closing, Ephraim's choice to share their story in this book transcends a mere recounting of events; it stands as a testament to the enduring impact of their lives. Their journey, rich with love and resilience, leaves an indelible mark not only on their children and grandchildren but on all who encounter their narrative.

This is more than a book; it's a beacon of wisdom and a guide on how to nurture and uphold the values that truly matter in life. As readers, we are invited to absorb these lessons and apply them in our own lives, ensuring that the essence of Ephraim and Sylvia's journey continues to inspire and resonate across generations.

Their story is a vivid reminder that the legacy we leave behind is sculpted by the love we share and the lives we touch along the way.

I, Ephraim, Take You, Sylvia,
To Be My Wife.
To Have And To Hold
From This Day Forward.
For Better, For Worse.
For Richer, For Poorer,
In Sickness And In Health,
To Love And To Cherish;
Until Death Do Us Part,
According To God's Holy Law.

Captured Memories

T HE PAGES THAT FOLLOW are a collection of treasured snapshots from the life of the Jones family. They highlight intimate family moments, joyous occasions shared with friends, and significant life events.

These images and stories reflect the strength of their family ties, the warmth of their friendships, and the profound influence they have had on one another's lives.

Alice Jones

Mother of Ephraim Jones
(photographed by Ephraim Jones)

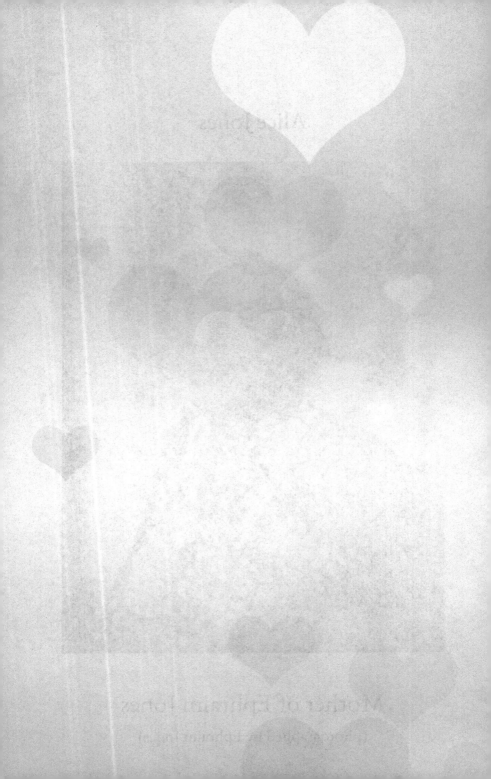

Alfred Jones

Father of Ephraim Jones

(photographed by Ephraim Jones)

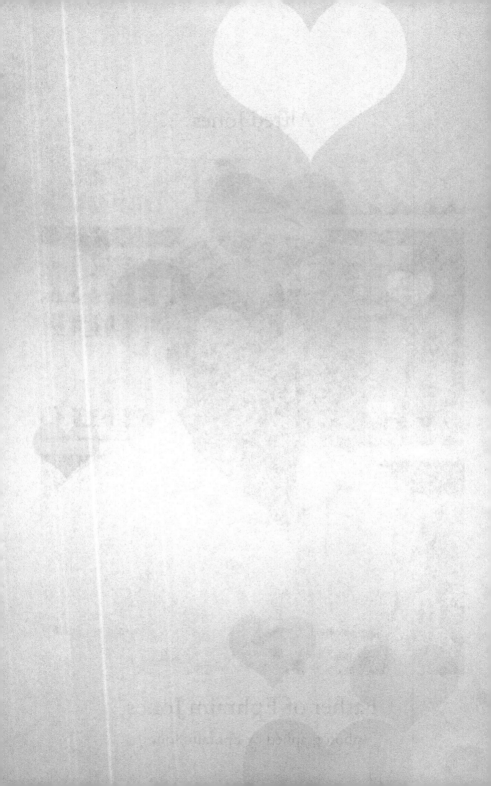

James & Violet Minns

Ephraim Jones & Sylvia Minns

Celebrating their Engagement
Yamacraw Beach; Nassau

Ephraim & Sylvia Jones

Wedding Day

(photographed by Rickey Wells)

Alfred & Alice Jones
(parents of the groom)

with

James & Violet Minns
(parents of the bride)

Ephraim & Sylvia's Wedding Day
Botanical Gardens; Nassau

(photographed by Rickey Wells)

Sylvia Jones

Dinner Date with Ephraim
Radisson Resort, Nassau
(photographed by Ephraim)

Ephraim & Sylvia Jones

Cruise Vacation (3rd)
St. Thomas & St. Maarten

Sylvia & Bunny

Bunny's 6th Birthday Party
Sea Floor Aquarium; Nassau
(photographed by Ephraim)

Sylvia Jones

Pregnant with Ja'Ronn
Family residence; Golden Gates I
(photographed by Ephraim)

Sylvia & Jamal Jones

(photographed by Ephraim)

Bunny, Ja'Ronn & Jamal Jones

The Jones' Children

(photographed by Ephraim)

Ja'Ronn Jones & Archdeacon Thompson

St. Anne's School Awards Day
(Mrs. Paul, Senior Mistress looking on)

(photographed by Ephraim)

Ephraim & Sylvia Jones

Dinner Date
Crystal Palace Hotel, Nassau

Ephraim, Sylvia & Ja'Ronn Jones
with
Aidan Alexander
(grandson)

Chucky Cheeses
Orlando, Florida

Ja'Ronn Jones

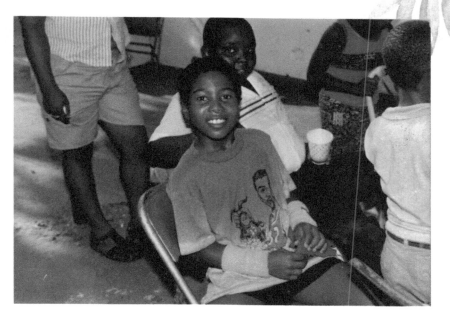

8 years old

Sylvia Jones
with
Bunny, Ja'Ronn & Jamal

Family Outing
Coral World, Nassau
(photographed by Ephraim)

Sylvia Jones

Dinner on Cruise Vacation
(photographed by Ephraim)

Ephraim, Sylvia, Bunny, Ja'Ronn & Jamal Jones
with
Alfred & Alice Jones (Ephraims parents)
&
Charles & Marilyn Colebrook (family friends)
&
Bridgett Francis (Bunny's friend)

Family Vacation Cruise

Bunny, Ja'Ronn & Jamal Jones
with
Alfred & Alice Jones (Ephraims parents)
&
Bridgett Francis (Bunny's friend)

Family Vacation Cruise

Ephraim, Sylvia & Ja'Ronn Jones

with

Aidan Alexander
(grandson)

Disney World
Orlando, Florida

Ephraim Jones "Grampy"

with

Aidan Alexander
(grandson)

(photographed by Jamal Jones)

Sylvia Jones
with
Resha, Reshia, Raquel Murphy
(granddaughters)

(photographed by Ephraim)

Jamaal & Ja'Ronn Jones
with
Alfred Jones
(grandfather)

At Belmont Abbey College
(photographed by Ephraim)

Sylvia & Ja'Ronn Jones

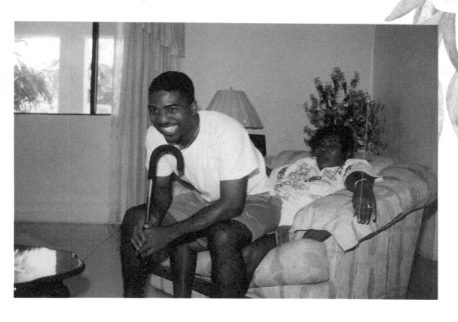

Special Moment
Family Residence, Nassau

(photographed by Ephraim)

Ephraim & Sylvia Jones

Ephraim's 50th Birthday Celebrations

(photographed by Tony Bethel)

Sylvia Jones

with

Craig & Stacy Segar
(family friends)

Jones Family Residence
Nassau

(photographed by Ephraim)

Sylvia Jones

with

Lorraine, Dawn & Lonnie Higgins
(close friends)

Sylvia Jones
with
Sonia Cox-Hamilton
(close friend)

Sonia's Wedding Day
(Sylvia served as Bridesmaid)

(photographed by Ephraim)

Sylvia Jones
with
Muhammad Ali

Las Vegas, Nevada

(photographed by Ephraim)

Ephraim & Sylvia Jones

with

Mrs. Lindroth
(family friend)

(photographed by Orjan Lindroth)

Sylvia Jones

with

Sonia Cox-Hamilton
(close friend)

&

Brenda, John & Melissa Trainor
(close friends)

(photographed by Ephraim)

Sylvia Jones
with
Amanda Lindroth
(close friend)

A Loving Embrace

Sylvia Jones

with

Lorraine Mullings
(close friend)

Ephraim & Sylvia Jones

Dinner at the Jones' Family residence
With family and friends including the
Lindroth family:
Orjan and his wife Amanda,
his mother and his sister Elizabeth

Ephraim & Jamal Jones

Father & Son Working Together
(2 Generations of Professional Photographers)
Atlantis Resort, Paradise Island

Sylvia & Jamal Jones

Family Dinner Outing

(photographed by Ephraim)

Ephraim & Sylvia Jones
with
Grandchildren

Christmas at the Jones' Family residence

(photographed by Jamal Jones)

Sylvia Jones

Shore Excursion
Vacation Cruise
(photographed by Ephraim)

Ephraim Jones
with
Bishop Walter & Sister Minalee Hanchell

Great Commission Ministries
Awarded Ephraim for
His Support Over The Years

Kim, Jamal, Rhyee, Ja-Ronn, Julianna, Jenifer and Sylvia

Christmas 2020

Ja-Ronn, Julianna, Jenifer, and Sylvia

Christmas 2020

Jamal, Rhylee, Kim, and Sylvia

Christmas 2020

Aidan, Jia, Julianna, and Ephraim

New Years Eve 2021

Jamal, Ephraim, Sylvia and Ja-Ronn

Sylvia and Granddaughters
Rhylee and Julianna

Jia, Sylvia and Julianna

Jia, Sylvia, Julianna, Aidan and Rhylee

Baby Jonathan

Julianna, Jonathan, Jia and Aidan

Honoring Sylvia's Legacy

♥

O N JANUARY 26, 2022, Sylvia Minns Jones concluded her valiant battle with cancer, departing this world peacefully. A month later, on February 24, 2022, she was laid to rest in a ceremony befitting her remarkable life.

The pages that follow contain the obituary from her funeral, a tribute to her enduring spirit and legacy.

A CELEBRATION OF THE LIFE OF

Sylvia Jones

Psalm 27:4
"One thing I ask of the Lord, this is what I seek,
that I may dwell in the house of the Lord all the days of my life
to gaze upon the beauty of the Lord and to seek him in his temple"

A Celebration for The Life of

Sylvia Jones

Born: June 5th, 1948 | Died: January 26th, 2022 | Age: 73 years

Service Held At:
THE REMNANT TABERNACLE OF PRAISE
Carmichael Road, Nassau, Bahamas

Thursday, February 24th, 2022 at 10:00 a.m.

Officiating:
Rev. Melvin Grant

Interment:
Woodlawn Gardens Cemetery
Soldier Road

Obituary

On June 5th, 1948 the late James and Violet Minns welcomed their first child, a beautiful girl whom they named Sylvia but affectionately called Syl. She was the eldest of six children.

Syl grew to be an ambitious, well groomed, determined and extremely talented lady. There was nothing she wanted, that her parents did not attempt to get, especially knowing it could lead to her empowerment. Syl loved to sew, bake and cook tasty dishes. Her specialty when it came to baking were rum and pina colada cakes and her Easter special…..mouthwatering hot cross buns.

Being an excellent seamstress Syl had the majority of Coconut Grove neighborhood business, mainly the sewing of school uniforms. No patterns were ever needed. Syl was excellent at what she did, going as far as designing and making her bridal dresses, mother and mother-in-law dresses, as well as her own wedding dress.

In 1967 two weeks after graduating from Aquinas College she was hired by Royal Bank of Canada as a bank teller. She moved up the ranks to a managerial position and eventually retired after 37 and a half years.

Syl met and fell in love with the man of her dreams, Ephraim Jones. On August 6th, 1976 Sylvia and Ephraim were joined in Holy Matrimony at Zion Baptist Church on East & Shirley Street.

On January 26th, 2022 at 5:21p.m. The Lord realized he needed another angel and called Sylvia home.

Her beautiful life will forever be cherished in the lives of her:

Husband: Ephraim Jones; sons: Ja-Ronn, Jenifer, Aidan, Jia & Julianna Jones, Jamal, Kimeish & Rhylee Jones; daughter: Kelly, Kirk, Re-Sha, Reshia, Richelle Rhea; brothers: James Jr, Arthur Minns; sisters: Agnes Ferguson, Maxine Curling, Diane Minns; brothers-in-law: Roscoe Ferguson, Ricardo Curling; sisters-in-law: Gladys Murphy, Guillimina Minns; nephews: Born Ferguson, Byron Ferguson (predeceased), Ashton Ferguson, Anvon Ferguson, Rickey Curling, Reno Curling, John Minns, Jordan Minns; nieces: Chandra Ferguson, Anya Ferguson, Sara Ferguson, Shayla Ferguson, Ka'Niska Curling; grandnieces: Saphirre, BreAnn, & Alivia Ferguson, Ricki, Castilla, Ria & Carder Curling; grandnephews: Cameron, Tsion & Bryson Ferguson, Keano & Castillo Curling; aunts: Merlene Smith Emma Rodriquez, Merlene Gilbert; uncle: Holman Gilbert; godchildren: Alexandria Richardson, Kendria Brown, Stevette Moncur, Charliss Bain-Josey, Ronesha Sands, Precious Stuart, Uriza Hutchenson, Geo Stubbs, CJ Bonaby, Duval Stubbs, Neveah Braynen, adopted sons: Franklyn Butler, Paul Walkine, Colin Jupp, Keno Turnquest, Delano & Omar Sands, Horatio Poitier
Other relatives and friends including Sonia Cox-Hamilton, Frank & Lorraine Mullings & family, Bertel & Barbara Holder & family, Latisha Curry, Karen Jarvis, Joy Khan, Shirley Smith, Janet Styles, Joy Taylor, Henry Storr & family, Vernal Sands, Charles & Marilyn Colebrooke & family, Alexander Gibson & family, Irvin & Kay Light-

1948 *Sylvia Jones* 2022

bourne & family, Geneva Aranha, Neville & Carol Braynen, Ken & Nellie Strachan, Caroline Turnquest, Dean & Mrs. Patrick Adderley, Dr. Charmaine Bodie, Elaine Pinder & family, Bishop Neil & Patrice Ellis, Bishop Walter & Melanie Hanchell, Ron & Noella Sands & family, Fr. Stephen & Italia Davies & family, Deacon Danny & Debrah Price, Dr. Harold & Moneira Munnings, Albert & Arthur Campbell, Derek & Patrice Dean & family, Carla Edwards & family, Thirza Dean, Maxine McCarthy, Sharon Wallace, Mona Culmer, Carla Wallace, Samuel & Annamae Strachan & family, Edward & Beryl Ferguson, Lee Munnings, Cyprianna Moss, Carolyn Stubbs, Rev. Melvin & Donna Grant, Marsha Adderley, Earle & Lenise Bethel, Calvin & Francise Greene, Clementine Butler, Eugiena Butler, Ereoshi Turnquest, Kimberley Cartwright, Helen Butler & family, Prescola Allen, David & Barbara Ferguson, Mr. & Mrs. Henry Dean, Destone & Shayna Ferguson, Minister Alfred & Marion Sears, Pedro & Sherry Rolle, Alfred & Bessley Gray, Dr. Derwin Munroe, Sis. Jackie Smith, William Wong, Jeffrey Pinder, Anand & Raquel Pinder, Rick Albury, Godfrey Forbes, Pauline Adderley, Francis Smith, Van & Ismae Deleveaux, Alex & Nadia Storr, Steven, Kim & Sandy Storr, Kingman & Leana P. Ingraham, Myles & Deidre Laroda, Mrs. Gordon, Mr. & Mrs. Luther Smith, Mother Stubbs, Peter & Sonia Turnquest, Mr. & Mrs. Malcolm Adderley, Mr. & Mrs. Adams, J.C. & Lorraine Smith, Dale Carey, Ravanna Mason, Mary Christie, Sunday McKenzie, David & Kelly Knowles, Mr. & Mrs. Crestwell Stuart, Steven & Della Moncur, Michael & Shenika Moss, Supt. Thompson & family, Fabian Fernander, Willamae McKenzie, Anthony & Joy Ecclestine, Kendal Jones, Roberta McKenzie, Patrick Ferguson, Sylvia Butler, Roger & Kevin Adderley, Prudence, Kelly, Florence & Elizabeth Murphy, Hettiemae Flowers, Frankiemae Moss and Alice Collie, Ray, Rodrick & Alfred Murphy, Camille, Edward & Michael Fields & family, Albertha W. Kemp, Berta Kemp, Rev. Dr. Tyrone & Doranda Jackson & family, Drs. Jackson & Unease Miller, Peterson & Patricia James, Rufus & Connie Kemp, Don Kemp, John & Yolanda Bonaby, Ian Thompson, Delphine Davis & family, Ian & Vanessa Lightbourne, Oral & Sabrina Martin, Slam & Della Moncur, Norys Cardoza, Santos Duarte, Kyle & Ashley Morejon, Jayden & Xavier Morejon, Kim & Toni Wilson, Gina Wilson & family, Gabriel & Clara Vasquez, Tyrone & Levaughn Cooper, Mr. & Mrs. Theo Taylor, Kirk & Angie Bethel, Mr. & Mrs. Anthony "Skeebo" Roberts, Rhyna Barry, Rev. & Mrs. Christopher King & family, Brett & Natasha Archer, Rev. & Mrs. J. Carl Rahming & family, Jermaine Higgs, Mr. & Mrs. Arnett, Falcon & Norma Watson, Cyprianna Stuart, David & Patrice Farrington, Larry Miller Ferguson, Raymond Miller, Mavis Brown, Adrianna Adderley, Cherene Carey, Chloe Knowles, Joanna Miller Nealy, Donna Miller, Melissa Miller-Deveaux, Delano Miller, Mr . & Mrs. Dan Knowles, Fred Munnings, Sir Michael Barnett, Orjan Lindroth (predeceased), Amanda, Eliza, Elizabeth & Magnus Lindroth, Jackie, Pamela & Neville Stubbs, Michael Hanna, Magical Beats Band, and numerous others.

Special thanks to the Staff of Residence Resort, 8th Bahamas Scout Troupe, Anglican Church Men, (Kevin Ryan, Godfrey Arthur, Fr. Bradley Miller, Joe Hamilton, Christian Knowles, Bertan Conyers, David & Darius Ferguson, Neil O'Brien, Everette Mackey, Clayton Curtis), "Lunch Bunch", Cleveland Clinic Oncology Department - Dr. Chieh-Lin Fu & Nurse Barbara, Royal Bank of Canada Retirees, Remnant Tabernacle of Praise, Bahamasair Stewardess BS: Wendy Humes, Annamae Maycock, Patricia Gibson-Sawyer & Anettrea Cargill, Bahamasair Porters Ft. Lauderdale: Robin Seepersad & Jerome, Josiah LeBlanc of Fred Hunters Funeral Service Ft. Lauderdale, FL., and Butler's Funeral Home.

ORDER OF SERVICE
Sylvia Jones

PRELUDE...R.T.O.P CHORAL

PRESIDING ....Deacon Neville Braynen

CALL TO WORSHIP / INVOCATION ....Pastor Melvin Grant

SELECTION .... Ismae Deleveaux

SCRIPTURE | 1 Corinthians 15: 50-58 ....Deaconess Annamae Strachan

CONGREGATIONAL HYMN.."Tis So Sweet To Trust In Jesus"

'Tis so sweet to trust in Jesus,
Just to take Him at His Word
Just to rest upon His promise,
Just to know, "Thus saith the Lord!"

Jesus, Jesus, how I trust Him!
How I've proved Him o'er and o'er
Jesus, Jesus, precious Jesus!
Oh, for grace to trust Him more!

I'm so glad I learned to trust Him,
Precious Jesus, Savior, Friend
And I know that He is with me,
Will be with me to the end.

Oh, how sweet to trust in Jesus,
Just to trust His cleansing blood
And in simple faith to plunge me
'Neath the healing, cleansing flood!

Yes, 'tis sweet to trust in Jesus,
Just from sin and self to cease
Just from Jesus simply taking
Life and rest, and joy and peace.

REFLECTIONS...Stephen Davies
Dr. Harry Munnings
Albert Campbell

THE REMNANT TABERNACLE OF PRAISE CHORAL

REFLECTIONS...Minister Alfred Sears

SCRIPTURE | Psalm 90: 1-12 ....Bishop Walter Hanchell

AS I KNEW HER ....Sonia Cox-Hamilton

SELECTION .... Debbie Price

CONDOLENCES ....Bishop Neil C. Ellis

SONG TRIBUTE

EULOGY ....Pastor Melvin Grant

PRAYER FOR THE FAMILY .... Deacon Danny Price (St. Cecilia)

RECESSIONAL HYMN..."When The Home Gates Swing Open"

I am on the upward road, leading to that bright abode,
Where forever my soul shall be free (be free);
Won't that be a happy time, heaven's bells will sweetly chime,
When the home gates swing open for me. (for me)

That will be a happy day,
When the clouds have passed away;
From my cares I shall be free,
When the home gates swing open for me.

Tho' sometime the path may lead thru the vale of sin and greed,
Jesus ever my refuge will be (will be);
Soon at home my trials o'er, I shall praise Him evermore.
When the home gates swing open for me.

I'll keep walking in His light, till my faith shall end in sight,
He will lead me till safe o'er the sea (the sea);
I shall find a welcome there, and a crown of glory wear,
When the home gates swing open for me.

TRIBUTES
Sylvia Jones

A Tribute to My Darling Wife "Syl-V"!

Sylvia, my Sugar Honey Bun, my Sweetie Pie, My Darling SJ, Sylvia Jones, Sylvia J, Lovely, Baby Doll, Sweet Potato Pie, Darling Heart!

These were some of the names I would call Syl at times. It was so funny that one of my grand-daughters said to me: "Grampa, what is Grammie Syl's real name, because you always calling her something different".

I laughed and said she is so sweet and juicy and delicious that I gave her a new name daily. My Syl-V was soo special!

Some of our friends call us the Bopsey Twins. My brother-in-law Arthur called us Starsky & Hutch, but whatever you call us we were inseparable.

About eight years ago, Syl became ill, we just could not figure out what was happening. We did everything we thought that could tell us what was going on with her, until one Sunday evening I finally convinced Syl to go to the hospital. I called one of her closest friends, Lorraine Mullings to let her know what was happening, and that was the start of my Sylvia's long journey with cancer.

But my tribute to her is about the wonderful person that she was, a fantastic wife, mother, grandmother, relative, colleague and my best friend.

There are so many wonderful friends and family who I can single out that have showed us love, compassion and support. To do that would no doubt offend some, because I might omit their names, even though they will always be a part of our journey.

My Syl-V was a blessing from God. Even today I still wondered what I did to deserve such a wonderful person to call my wife. Our relationship started off so beautiful and filled with so many wonderful memories.

This past Super bowl was the first time that we did not watch the game together. She was a part of me, and I was a part of her. She can never be replaced. I want to live on with her memory and be grateful for the blessings that she left, our children and now our grandchildren.

My Syl-V made so many friends during her time on this earth. For the first time, I got to see for myself how much she meant to so many. With the outpouring of love and support from friends, family and even strangers, I realized that My Syl-V was an angel sent here to be a blessing.

We all will miss her, but we are comforted in knowing that she lived a good life and left a legacy for all of us. Yes, we mourn her passing but we rejoice in her life. And although we consider it short-lived, she did so much for so many while she was here.

My Syl-V has gone on to her glory, and there is no question in anyone's mind that she is not in the arms of our Lord. She loved life, she loved her family, she loved her friends, and she loved her customers. She loved all of us and she lived that kind of life filled with love and compassion.

My Syl-V has left us, but she has left so much with us and for that we eternally grateful for a life well lived. Sleep on my dear, I loved you dearly, but we know our Creator loves you even more and He called you home to be with him.

We will see you again!

1948 Sylvia Jones 2022

My "big baby"....words I will never hear you say again. Just so you know, I am my Mom's "favorite"! Even though I was "the favorite" my mother showed us love equally and was always fair. She was present for all occasions, especially birthdays. 9th Terrace was where the entire family would all meet to cut cake, do the "dolphin", the electric slide and have a great time.

The memories I have of you and what you meant to me will forever be engraved in my mind and in my heart. I am so blessed and grateful that you had the opportunity to know and love your precious Rhy Rhy. Rhylee reminds me of you daily. She is still here pushing your walker around the house and has now claimed it as hers since you aren't sitting in it.

Mummy, I never could've imagined my world with you in it. I will always admire your strength and resilience. I still remember when the doctor returned to your room and said, "Mrs. Jones, you have cancer". My knees buckled and I held onto the bed. You looked at me and said "it's alright".

You were in pain daily but you never let that keep you down. You wanted to live and that you did.

Baking, cooking and shopping were your favorite pastimes. I could clearly remember days while driving you to chemo you would always say, "Mally when we leave I want to go to one store". I always knew it was never going to be just one store and Bealls was always the first stop. You would always try to bribe me with "lunch" once we were done, but most times lunch became dinner because of the amount of time you would spend shopping.

Mummy, none of us wanted you to leave but you were tired and in need of rest. I am so grateful you were chosen to be my Mother and even more grateful for the memories we have shared.

Love you always,
"Your Mally"

Farewell Big Sis

The death of our beloved sister Sylvia has certainly pierced our hearts. Syl was our motivator, our run to person whenever we heard NO from our parents. She led the way for us in the Minns household, the first born, first to graduate high school, Aquinas College to be exact and within two weeks of graduating she gained employment at Royal Bank of Canada, Bay Street in 1967, until she retired in 2001.

Syl was also the first among the siblings to purchase a vehicle, a red Maverick, which we all cherished, especially Agnes, who became a very happy driver. Syl cared deeply for her siblings; of course we had our share of disagreements, unlike some families I suppose. We even stayed clear of each other for very long periods of time, but nevertheless, that bonding of love remained strong, and kept us connected. Syl gave us our first niece Kelly, who we cherished and affectionately called Bunny. For us girls she was our first human doll. Then along came our nephews Ja-Ronn and Jamal who we loved none the less. The growth of all our children proves how important and expensive TIME is, and how fast it goes by.

Therefore we, her sisters, are focusing on maintaining the strong family bond. It's so unfortunate that we had to lose our loved one to that deadly cancerous blood disease, called multiple myeloma, but we find comfort just knowing her pain is no more. So until we meet again Big Sis be our guardian Angel, direct our path and protect us from every form of evil, and ill will.

Forever in our hearts Maxine, Diane & Agnes

1948 Sylvia Jones 2022

TRIBUTE TO MY LIFELONG FRIEND SYL

Syl has been in my life so long it seems like forever and I am missing her voice and her presence so much. I met this beautiful soul in 1967 when I entered Royal Bank of Canada as a new employee she impressed me then and even now.

She was gifted in her hands, mind and spirit.

Hands: She sewed free hand, anything from dresses to pants to curtains to masks. Many of us got masks from her
Mind: She was strong willed and inherited her father's personality
        She was kind and inherited her mother's gentle ways
        She was focused and quick with figures and with her tongue
        She spoke her mind without fear
Hands: Syl's cooking was legendary and was only eclipsed by her awesome baking talents
Spirit: She never let obstacles stand in her way
        She overcame them
        She never complained throughout her eight-year battle with Cancer!!
        She stayed positive and would bake cakes to take to the doctors and nurses at Cleveland Clinic
        She loved her family and friends and showed it whenever she was able
        She became a sister to me and I to her
        We talked about everything and she was a joy to be around

Although I am sad she is no longer with us, I am happy she is out of her pain and more importantly, that she had time to "pack for her destination"

Thanks forever!!
Sonia Cox-Hamilton

GRAVESIDE HYMNS
Sylvia Jones

I'LL FLY AWAY

Some glad morning when this life is o'er;I'll fly away;
To a home on God's celestial shore,I'll fly away.

I'll fly away, O glory, I'll fly away,
When I die, hallelujah by and by, I'll fly away.

When the shadows of this life have gone, I'll fly away.
Like a bird from prison bars has flown, I'll fly away.

Just a few more weary days and then, I'll fly away.
To a land where joys shall never end, I'll fly away.

THAT GLAD REUNION DAY

There will be a happy meeting in heaven I know,
When we see the many loved ones
we've known here below,
Gather on the blessed hill-tops with hearts all aglow.
That will be a glad reunion day.

Glad day, a wonderful day,
Glad day, a glorious day
There with all the holy angels and loved ones to stay,
That will be a glad reunion day.

There within the holy city we'll sing and rejoice,
Praising Christ the blessed Saviour
with heart and with voice
Tell him how we came to love Him
and make Him our choice.
That will be a glad reunion day.

When we live a million years in that wonderful place,
Basking in the love of Jesus, beholding His face.
It will seem but just a moment of praising His grace.
That will be a glad reunion day.

IT IS WELL WITH MY SOUL

When peace, like a river, attendeth my way
When sorrows, like sea billows, roll
Whatever my lot, Thou hast taught me to say
It is well, It is well with my soul

It is well, with my soul
It is well, it is well with my soul

Though Satan should buffet though trials should come
Let this blest assurance control
That Christ has regarded my helpless estate
And hath shed His own blood for my soul

My sin O the bliss of this glorious tho't
My sin not in part but the whole
Is nailed to His cross, and I bear it no more
Praise the Lord, praise the Lord, O my soul!

For me, be it Christ, be it Christ hence to live!
If Jordan above me shall roll,
No pang shall be mine, for in death as in life,
Thou wilt whisper Thy peace to my soul.

But Lord, 'tis for Thee, for Thy coming we wait;
The sky, not the grave, is our goal;
Oh, trump of the angel! Oh, voice of the Lord!
Blessed hope! blessed rest of my soul.

1948 Sylvia Jones 2022

Pallbearers

Charles Colebrooke	Dr. Harold Munnings
Bjorn Ferguson	Franklyn Butler
Keno Turnquest	Charles Colebrooke Jr.

Honourary Pallbearers

Arthur Minns
Pedro Rolle
Derek Dean
Brent Archer
Calvin Greene
Alexander Gibson
Colin Jupp

Acknowledgement

We, the family of the late Sylvia Jones wish to extend our heartfelt gratitude to our family and friends and are deeply indebted for your constant prayers, personal visits, telephone calls and other acts of kindness, especially your support here today. We thank you for helping us bear our sorrow in this our time of bereavement. May God bestow His richest blessings upon you!

The Family

www.sylviajones.net

Ephraim Jones

Ephraim Jones is an outstanding Bahamian and community figure.

He was born and raised in New Providence, The Bahamas, in the Chippingham community, where he resides to this day.

He became a Boy Scout at an early age. While many do not continue past childhood, Ephraim, affectionately known as "Skip" by Scouts, dedicated his life to the organization. He has led countless troops, leading young boys to become fine young men. These men still consider him as a father figure today, girded with strong morals, a mindset of self-sufficiency and community service.

His sons, Ja'Ronn and Jamal can attest to his outstanding character in the home as well. He poured unconditional love into them, along with his wife Sylvia, now deceased.

A photographer by trade, Ephraim has captured some of the most significant people and events in The Bahamas. For many years, he also owned a photo laboratory, before the digital age.

Today, he continues professional photography, but he has also found another love.

He successfully operates the Residence Resort in the Garden of Eden, Eastwood Estates, Nassau. Its restaurant is well known for having some of the best Bahamian food in the country.

Ephraim remains committed to God, his family, and his country. He is elated to have published his first book and has intentions of producing more in the future, including sharing rare photos he captured over time.

A. Felicity Darville

A. Felicity Darville began writing in earnest at her primary school, Temple Christian, and then her high school, St. Augustine's College, where she assisted in writing pieces for her school, as well as writing and delivering powerful motivational speeches. Since then, she has become a well-noted professional writer.

She co-authored the inspiring anthology "Keep Going", published by Universal Impact Press, and she has assisted many others in writing and editing their own books.

She has a popular news column called "Face to Face with Felicity" which is published each Tuesday in The Tribune newspaper and is found online at tribune242.com.

Felicity is also an extraordinary radio and television broadcaster, and has covered numerous national and international events. She has even served as host or mistress of ceremonies for some of these high-level events.

She has used her media platform as a tool for advocacy to help bring about change in her country. She was awarded by the Bahamas National Breastfeeding Association, the Disabled Persons Organization, and the Bahamas Alliance for the Blind and Visually Impaired for her advocacy work, which has resulted in policy and legislative changes. In 2021, she received the Icon of the Year award for Media Advocacy, and in 2018, she received a PAHO award for health reporting during the Bahamas Press Club Awards.

Felicity is married to Victor Darville, and they graduated from the Bahamas Agriculture and Marine Science Institute in 2023 with Associate of Science Degrees in Aquaculture.

Her children: Ras Elijah; Malia; Ras Jesse; Kindy Emmanuel; Victory; and Victorious; as well as her granddaughter Kae'Lynn are her constant sources of inspiration.

She lives a God-centered life and is devoted to her family. She loves her country, The Bahamas, and is focused on the environment; sustainability; agriculture and fisheries; youth empowerment; human rights; and women's affairs.

Acknowledgements

Special Thanks to:

The Butler family, especially our adopted son, Frank Butler, and his family Eugenia

Felicity and mother Clementine Butler

The entire staff at Butler's Funeral Home

Canon Stephen Davies & family

Dereck Dean & family

Dr. Harry Munnings & family

The Anglican Church Men

Alexander Gibson & family

Godfrey Arthur

Henry Dean

Kevin Ryan

Christian Knowles

Lorraine & Frank Mullings

Sonia Hamilton & family

Joy Khann

The Lindroth family, especially Amanda and Orjan Lindroth

Magnus Lindroth (the first time I entered the Savoy Theatre was thanks to him!)

Deacon Danny & Debbie Price

Ismae & Edison Deleveaux, Jr.

Marsha Adderley

Dr. Charmaine Bodie, Sylvia's adopted daughter

Supt. Sean Thompson

Hon. Alfred Sears & family

The family of Henry F. Storr

My brothers and sisters-in-law including: James Minns, Agnes Ferguson, Maxine Curling, Arthur Minns, and Dianne Minns

Arthur and Albert Campbell

Brent Archer & family

Beryl Ferguson

Hon. V. Alfred Gray & family

Dr. Michael Spencer & family

Dr. Derwin, Lance & Leslie Munroe

Pastor Melvin Grant & the Remnant Tabernacle of Praise

Ingrid Rose & family

Ken & Nellie Strachan

Calvin Greene & family

The wonderful staff at The Residence Resort & Garden of Eden

Vernal Sands

Bishop Neil Ellis & family

Bishop J. Carl Rahming

Ron Sands & family

Camille Fields & family

Irwin Lightbourne & family

Bishop Walter & Sister Minalee Hanchell

Mona Maria Culmer

Michael Hanna & Magical Beats Band

Mother Helen Butler & family

William Wong

David Knowles & family

Neillie & Ken Strachan

Barbara & Bertell Holder

Nurse Letitia Curry

Karon Javis

All of our Godchildren - we love you all

Mrs. Minnis

Mr. & Mrs. Winston Davis

Ian & Vanessa Thompson

Chef Edwin Johnson & family

Cyprianna Moss

Geneva Aranha

Winston Davis and family

Carole & Neville Brennen

Lenora Munnings

Lenora Archer, Assistant Book Editor

From the three men in Sylvia's life: her husband Ephraim and sons Jamaal and Ja-Ronn, we wish to extend heartfelt thanks to all of our family, friends, and loved ones who have supported and strengthened us.

To all we may have inadvertently left out, we offer our hearts full of sincere gratitude.

Your love and encouragement has been the wind beneath our wings!

UNIVERSAL IMPACT PRESS

Made in the USA
Columbia, SC
10 October 2024

43404657R00143